T0295644

"If you already think you know what organizing is, think again. Let one of the most creative organization theorists of the last forty years open your mind and enjoy feeling your brain heat up. There is political urgency here too, because if we don't start thinking and doing organization differently then our planet will become too lively for us to live on. Read this book."

Martin Parker, Professor of Organization
Studies and Lead for the Bristol Inclusive
Economy Initiative, Bristol University, UK

"In this highly informative, provocative, and passionate book, Gibson Burrell challenges what is presented as organization theory, demanding of us the bravery to examine and question the organizational consequences of the ways in which, and by which, we live. Go on. Challenge yourself!"

Barbara Townley, Emeritus Professor,
School of Management, University of
St Andrews, UK

"Never judge a book by its cover. Behind an innocent title, Gibson Burrell shows us why organizational scholars must dissolve the many neo-institutionalist smokescreens that mask the ugly realities of corporate life, and why we must never stop scrutinizing how power is exercised from the inner vestiges of organizations, or exploring what can be done about it. With remarkable wit and edge, this book reminds us why Burrell remains one of the most important voices in business education and critique."

Torkild Thanem, Professor of
Management & Organization Studies,
Stockholm University, Sweden

Organization Theory

This shortform book presents an overview of theoretical and empirical work in the field of organization theory. In doing so, it provides both a critical analysis of the state of knowledge in the field and offers recommendations for future directions.

It is about both thinking differently and considering what is already known within Organization Theory. With coverage of the foundations of organization studies, the importance of bureaucracy, and insights into institutional approaches, the book also makes space to consider the key role of alternatives in the development of the field. A panoply of modes of organizing the modern economy and civil society have arisen wherein it is often said that the platform has replaced the pyramid. Yet, in 2022, the Covid-19 pandemic underscores the state's responsibility to maintain public health through centralized and coherent organization rather than outsourcing, subcontracting, and the gig economy. This book offers a new direction for research focusing upon 'organizational camouflage,' where the unmasking of the large hierarchical corporation's enduring role in governing our everyday lives would become Organization Theory's revelatory task.

Organization Theory: A Research Overview will be of value to researchers, scholars, and students in the fields of business and management, especially those interested in the intersection of politics and organizations.

Gibson Burrell is Professor of Organization Theory at the University of Manchester, UK.

State of the Art in Business Research
Series Editor: Geoffrey Wood

Recent advances in theory, methods, and applied knowledge (alongside structural changes in the global economic ecosystem) have presented researchers with challenges in seeking to stay abreast of their fields and navigate new scholarly terrains.

State of the Art in Business Research presents shortform books which provide an expert map to guide readers through new and rapidly evolving areas of research. Each title will provide an overview of the area, a guide to the key literature, and theories and time-saving summaries of how theory interacts with practice.

As a collection, these books provide a library of theoretical and conceptual insights, and exposure to novel research tools and applied knowledge, that aid and facilitate in defining the state of the art, as a foundation stone for a new generation of research.

Gossip, Organization and Work
A Research Overview
Kathryn Waddington

Remote Working
A Research Overview
Alan Felstead

Business History
A Research Overview
John F. Wilson, Ian G. Jones, Steven Toms, Anna Tilba, Emily Buchnea, and Nicholas Wong

Complexity in Organizations
A Research Overview
Stig O. Johannessen

Organization Theory
A Research Overview
Gibson Burrell

For more information about this series, please visit: www.routledge.com/State-of-the-Art-in-Business-Research/book-series/START

Organization Theory
A Research Overview

Gibson Burrell

Routledge
Taylor & Francis Group

LONDON AND NEW YORK

First published 2022
by Routledge
4 Park Square, Milton Park, Abingdon, Oxon OX14 4RN

and by Routledge
605 Third Avenue, New York, NY 10158

Routledge is an imprint of the Taylor & Francis Group, an informa business

British Library Cataloguing-in-Publication Data
A catalogue record for this book is available from the British Library

Library of Congress Cataloging-in-Publication Data
Names: Burrell, Gibson, author.
Title: Organization theory: a research overview / Gibson Burrell.
Description: Abingdon, Oxon; New York, NY: Routledge, 2022. |
Series: State of the art in business research | Includes bibliographical
references and index.
Identifiers: LCCN 2022002649 (print) | LCCN 2022002650 (ebook) |
ISBN 9780367713638 (hbk) | ISBN 9780367713652 (pbk) |
ISBN 9781003150503 (ebk)
Subjects: LCSH: Organizational sociology–Research.
Classification: LCC HM786 .B86 2022 (print) | LCC HM786 (ebook) |
DDC 302.3/5–dc23/eng/20220125
LC record available at https://lccn.loc.gov/2022002649
LC ebook record available at https://lccn.loc.gov/2022002650

ISBN: 978-0-367-71363-8 (hbk)
ISBN: 978-0-367-71365-2 (pbk)
ISBN: 978-1-003-15050-3 (ebk)

DOI: 10.4324/9781003150503

Typeset in Times New Roman
by Deanta Global Publishing Services, Chennai, India

FOR THE USUAL 'BIG BURRELL' SUSPECTS

Clare, Anna, Katy, Rosie, and Owain
and those with whom they lovingly share their lives

Contents

Acknowledgement

I have been very fortunate in my career to have worked with some truly remarkable people. Some have even been academics. My thanks go here to my friends and colleagues who were made redundant at the same time as myself by the School of Business at the University of Leicester. Our 'sin' was to engage in the study of critical management studies using ideas from political economy. The organizational analysis of our nine months of resistance and the reprehensible behaviour of senior management in the institution is a publication that lies in the future. The fortitude and organizational abilities of my colleagues in 2021 made the experience more bearable than it might and it was even enjoyable on occasion. To them I offer my sincere thanks.

1 From the Personal to the Political

The Personal

This is a small book about both thinking differently, *and* legitimating what is already known, upon a large canvas about politics and organizations and the lives of individuals across the globe. I hope you will forgive me if I stray here for a moment at the beginning of this analysis to consider the individual I know best, but, of course, by no means completely. That is, myself. I am telling you this, dear reader, because this is a book on the *current* state of research in, and ideas about, Organization Theory. This is a text written for 2022 but history, some of it personal, is always relevant to anyone's understanding, whether they are the writer or the reader of a particular text. It would be nice to be able to say the book has been an objective survey of the field, totally free of particular prejudices, slants, positionings, and politico-ideological bias. I cannot say that – but neither can anyone else writing such an overview – anywhere. In any discipline. My particular standpoint, which has pervaded this work, is based upon 56 years of thinking about organizations and organizing – and this is why we go back to a cold November day in London, which is a city in the south-east corner of the UK.

I became seriously interested in organizations and organizing on November 10, 1965. London is 300 miles from my home village and so I had taken the overnight bus to the metropolis. I had an interview booked for 11am at the London School of Economics, Department of Sociology, to see whether they would have me as an undergraduate student. I was 17 years old. After meeting my sister and her husband for breakfast, they put me on a 'Tube' to a station near the LSE. This was about 10am and the underground was relatively quiet after rush hour. The train came to a halt at its third stop and I was sitting with the arch of the tube wall on my left. The platform was on my right. I heard a choked word to my left. It was 'Help'. There was one other person in my part of the Tube but he seemed oblivious to the cry. I heard it again, a little louder this time. Suddenly, between me

DOI: 10.4324/9781003150503-1

and the tiled wall a head appeared, shouting for help. I remember it was a white woman but cannot recall age nor anything else of her appearance. I jumped up and went to the door of the carriage which was still open. A London Underground worker was about to signal the train off from the platform. I shouted out that 'there's someone trapped on the other side of the train'. So, the employee yelled out down the platform 'Joe, cut the juice'. She then came into our carriage and saw the trapped person through the window. She said loudly and forcefully to me and the few other people in the carriage 'Get off the train, get away from the platform, and leave the station'. She had spoken not one word of comfort to the trapped woman. She did not approach her, nor engage in eye contact, nor indicate help was close at hand. To this day I do not know the fate of the fallen woman, why she was on the wrong side of the platform, had she jumped or tripped, or how (indeed if) she was rescued. In confronting the callousness of the staff of the London Underground, I did as I was told and surfaced in a part of London I knew not.

At this point, shock had set in, yet my concern was to reach the LSE by 11am. I had absolutely no idea where I was in Central London nor where the School was. At this time, on British TV, the police were presented as caring local 'bobbies' who would always be there to assist members of the public. So, I approached an officer standing on a street corner by himself. I began 'I'm looking for the London School of Economics'. Before I could explain what had happened, he said 'Fuck off, sonny, I'm busy'. My first confrontation, therefore, with the Metropolitan Police was not a happy one and it did little to stem my rising sense of panic.

I eventually reached the LSE at about 11.10am and found the Sociology Department. I knocked on the door of the interviewing lecturer at 11.20. He looked decidedly discommoded and asked me to sit down so, without invitation to speak, I blurted out the events of the morning on my tube journey. I suggested (without evidence) that it might have been an attempted suicide. My regional accent was even stronger than usual as, somewhat relieved, I thought there would be some understanding of what was, for me, a significant metropolitan trauma. He barely looked at me and heard my blurted story without any apparent interest. He then asked, 'why do you want to read sociology?' He never went off script after that. There was no recognition of me being a human under stress – just a desire to run through the formal selection process in a mechanical way, sticking to the abbreviated timetable. Later that week, I was to discover that I would not be offered a place at the LSE.

So, on November 10, 1965, I interacted with members of three London based organizations; London Underground, the Metropolitan Police, and the London School of Economics and Political Science. On the bus journey home, my feeling was that these large organizations were unlike what I had imagined them to be. Prestigious, high profile, based in the capital, and very well resourced, they appeared – shockingly – not to be interested in the real lives of those they 'served'. Indeed, by virtue of their unfeelingness, they did not seem to think that service was an issue for them at all. From that point on, I became interested to learn about these objects of power and why and how they operated as they did. These sorts of organizations were problematised for me from that day on. They became my theoretical object – the object of my interest – and not necessarily in any effort to support their everyday activities. There was no wish on my part to aid their work, for I saw them as politically motivated agents, exercising power over those people with whom they came into contact. I still do.

The Political

By going back 55 years, we turn back to a time when 'organization' was a relatively unproblematic notion (Selznick 1948; Dale 1959; Etzioni 1960; Metcalfe and Urwick 2004; Hinings and Meyer 2018). In Britain and across the world (Guillen 1994a,b, 2010), the Second World War had demonstrated that nation states who embraced both the 'warfare state' and the 'welfare state' had a chance of survival. The organization of the war effort using mass production techniques, mass mobilization of labour (Huxley 1943; Smith 2006), social protection of the workforce, and a commitment to 'total war' through almost complete administration of the economy and the polity was central to victory or defeat (Bauman 2000). The concentration of power in the hands of a centralized state bureaucracy was obvious and in the mid-1960s Keynesianism was relatively unquestioned as *the* way in which economies were run. This required state intervention on a very large scale as day-to-day management of the economic system was seen as essential. Everywhere one looked, the warfare and the welfare state had thrown up a field of organizing as far as the eye could see (Albrow 1970; Whitley 1999; Aglietta 2000; Boyer 2005).

I took an undergraduate course in the late 1960s given by Nicos Mouzelis based on his book *Organization and Bureaucracy*. Here the existence of organization was taken for granted and Mouzelis was seeking to show the Weberian roots of Organization Theory coming into full flower. This made a lot of sense in explaining the then current landscape. Subsequently, my PhD was supervised by Tom Lupton who said one day in 1972 that I should recognize that 'Industrial Sociology is dead. It is being replaced everywhere by organizational sociology. Industry is dying in Britain but management is everywhere'. This was a prescient prediction from someone who, as Dean of one of the UK's two Business Schools at the time, should be well placed to know about Britain's trajectory and that of his discipline. Some 50 years later, what do we face if we survey the field? Today, very troublingly, we have to ask the question 'Has the concept of "organization" even got a future?'.

The collective future of the discipline appears to be under threat in the face of severe questioning of our work, sometimes even by those inside the tent (Williamson 1993; Swedberg 2003; Rowlinson 1996, 2004; Oswick et al. 2011; DiMaggio and Powell 2000). *Organization Theory: A Research Overview* has been written, in part, to provide a defence of the discipline and to show how its relevance is centrally important in the face of attacks upon it which are eating into its fabric. This fragmentation began in recent years and the pace of it is accelerating. Before long, the discipline of Organization Studies (OS) will be, at best, a mere adjunct to conventional management studies, taught sparingly on the fringes of programmes and courses, with a diminished sense of itself as a vibrant entity and of its putative role in academic life (Contu 2009). It will have been forced into the margins, as a twilight teaching subject, devoid of any gravitas. Organization Theory, however, should not be at the edge of business and management studies. It should be at its very heart, pumping discontent through the veins and arteries of the body of the discipline. But, as I have discovered, along with friends and close colleagues in Leicester University, this exhibition of discontent with one's 'betters', any critique of their methods and ethics, any investigation of their lack of financial acumen, and all attempts to analyse their inadequacies are frowned upon by those in senior management who appear to know nothing of academic values, save for their own power to defend the indefensible and curtail academic freedom.

As we begin this book then, it felt necessary to point out to the reader that, whatever one thinks, the personal is the political (Marsden 2005). They are inextricably intertwined. I have happened to be associated during my career with permanent posts within three departments that previously might have laid claim to being centres of Organization Studies, or more narrowly with Organization Theory. These are Warwick Business School, Alliance Manchester Business School (which merged with UMIST some time ago), and the University of Leicester. Martin Parker has subjected two of these institutions to an organizational analysis (Parker 2014, 2021) of their own. Within these institutions, it was the 'political' rationale for contracting Organization Theory that held sway, for what people in the area did was to frighten senior management, sometimes even intentionally. Our internal critique of their style of managing, tinged with trade unionism, and the connections we made to other managerial approaches that were possible and preferable, appeared threatening. For those Deans and Heads of School seeking a legitimatory device to shift resources towards 'strategy', 'organizational psychology', 'behavioural science', and 'service operations management', all of which are a little devoid of institutional 'edginess', their time had come. Organization Theory, motivated by a critical edge, and analysis directed on occasion towards its place of employment (Fournier and Grey 2000), suggested that its purveyors were non-malleable and somewhat dangerous to the organizations that housed it. Opportunism, evidenced in business schools and universities intending to remove this sort of internal critique, has been very evident in recent years. Contextually, the 'culture wars' within the UK allow the critique of subjects based upon the arts, humanities, and social studies (not social *sciences*) to bloom. It is not a good time in the UK higher education sector to be STEMless and to have one's legitimacy questioned (Contu 2009; Fleming 2021) by those with institutional power.

The institutional processes at work are not identical in those universities mentioned above (Townley 1997) but they function manifestly to encourage the diminution of the critical masses that have fostered the development of Organization Theory, both nationally and internationally. The working conditions of senior staff are worsened and the re-labelling of their expertise gets under way, so their voice is no longer attended to. Their role on committees is ended. Feeling powerless, or shown the door, they leave in droves. Young members of the profession are told there is no room for them on full-time staff and their progress through probation made impossible. They leave in droves. Established lecturers are not put forward for promotion by their deans and are told to their face that their value is limited. At all levels, academic staff seek (most often successfully) institutional exit (Fleming 2019, 2021). But, often, in their haste, they do not translocate to an alternative, large, growing centre of scholarship. They find places where Organization Theory is tolerated in small doses. Tolerated, not as large concentrations of questioning, motivated researchers in which politicized attitudes and values are seen as having a once respectable lineage, but as typically made up of troublemakers and 'refusers'. Almost everywhere, the Business School seems to be out of love with Organization Studies – assuming, of course, that such a state ever existed.

But many in Organization Studies are out of love with the Business School (Taylor 2012; Fleming 2014, 2019). Most noticeable of those, perhaps, is Martin Parker who has spoken of 'fucking management' (2001) and of 'shutting down the Business School' (2018). These terms are not likely to endear anyone speaking on these issues, with such a vocabulary, to senior management both in Schools of Management and the offices of the Vice Chancellor, but they are indicative of mutual feelings of distaste and anxiety. So, Organization Theorists are unhappy with the organizations in which they live. But isn't everyone? (Brignall 2021, p. 31).

Sketching the Field

There is no way in a book of 35,000 words that one can describe, let alone analyse, all that is going on in the field of Organization Theory. So, this author, unrepentantly motivated by feelings of distaste for many senior management cadres, built up by being a university manager for over 16 years and seeing 'inside the belly of the beast', will focus only upon certain elements within my discipline, attempting to look back at what has been achieved but also forward to what might be done. The structure will be built around the following interconnected themes which largely (though not entirely) parallel the chapters:

- **Definitional Issues**
  - What is an organization?
  - What is organizing?
  - What is Organization Theory?
- **Methodological Issues**
  - Dialectics and the transcendence of binaries
- **Conceptual Issues**
  - Conventional understandings of Organization Theory
  - What lies outside of conventional Organization Theory?
  - How to widen conventional Organization Theory
- **Political and Philosophical Issues**
  - What *can* organizations do and what *do* organizations do?
  - How do organizations relate to the world?

These will be sections and chapters of different length. The book has a full bibliography at the end for the old-fashioned reader (like myself) but at this point I begin with the issue of what is an organization?

2 What Is an Organization?

'Organization' has a long history as a term (Cummings and Thanem 2002), taking the user back to Romano-Greek times where 'organon' meant a musical instrument, a weapon, or a tool of some kind. Its meaning transmogrifies over the centuries within Europe. Today, it is both a noun and a verb and so we face difficulties at the outset in agreeing our terms. It is defined in the OED, for example, as both 'the condition of being organized' **and** 'the way in which something is organized'. It is the action of 'putting into systematic form', 'the arrangement and coordination of parts', an 'organized structure, body or being'. As a noun it is 'an organized body, system or society'. It is something 'formed into a whole with mutually connected parts that are dependent upon each other'. It attains 'an orderly structure that is in working order' dependent upon 'vital processes' that are 'systematically arranged'. Its breadth of meaning has been a boon to those seeking a wide area of intellectual coverage and a curse to those seeking precision.

What is 'organization' and why does it matter has been the subject matter of many founders of Organization Theory (Selznick 1948; Etzioni 1960; Dale 1959; Mouzelis 2017). Looking at the dates of these publications one can see that 'organization' comes to the fore as a term of conceptual utility after World War II. This is because, in order to survive the move to 'total war', nation states and their suppliers of munitions, manpower and womanpower, and manipulation of the populace required a move to the full bureaucratization of society (Thompson 1956; Wittfogel 1957; Schofield 2001). The regime of economic and social control in the 'successful' war time nations was highly organized by being highly bureaucratic. But whilst the warfare and welfare economies that rely upon bureaucratic modes of domination within the state came to the fore in the 1940s, they almost immediately came under attack from anti-state thinkers (Huxley 1943; Selznick 1948; Hayes 2008). This form of centralized organizing was seen as slow, hesitant, and inefficient (Clegg and Dunkerley 1980; Williamson 1993). It held back progress in technological developments because of the vested

DOI: 10.4324/9781003150503-2

interests that formed around fixed organizational structures and tight control systems. The organization in its bureaucratic form was seen as a block to the development of advanced consumer capitalism.

But, in late 2019, the world became aware of something 'natural' that threatened the maintenance of socio-economic normality and raised the issue in the next two years of how 'organizing' against the 'organism' might be achieved.

The Pandemic

This is a book written in the second year of the Covid-19 pandemic. In the fourteenth century across Europe, perhaps a third of the population died from bubonic plague (Theilmann and Cate 2007). In southern Europe it was closer to a half. This massive demographic shift changed the social and economic world dramatically. It became organized differently. When the plague visited Britain again in 1665, within the village of Eyam in the county of Derbyshire, the population was virtually wiped out and all age groups were affected. Whole families died within weeks, or even days, of first infection. Yet they endured voluntary quarantine. The word 'crisis' is much overused but plague years did demonstrate that the line between life and death (the moment of 'crisis') was easily crossed by members of a population if quarantines were not respected. But the presence of many deaths is a great opportunity for the living to think and do differently (Kuhn 1970). In the Black Death of the fourteenth century, the peasants of Britain and in many countries across Europe succeeded in throwing off serfdom (McLynn 2012) perhaps because of huge labour shortages. According to McLynn (2012: 61–2), in England *before* the spread of the plague, when an unfree peasant died, a fine had to be paid to the lord to continue the tenancy, his best beast was given to the lord and his second-best beast to the parson to pay for the funeral. A fine was to be paid to have a daughter enter into marriage, or for the family to move villages. Four days labour per fortnight were to be levied by the landowner. It was this unfree regime that changed, at least in part for the better, in the late fourteenth century after the Black Death. And what might we expect after Covid-19 where the UN believes, so far, a minimum of 5 million people have died in the pandemic?

Anyone looking out of their window in the last 12 months, across many parts of the world, might have had an opportunity to think about the issues of political economy which are involved in closing down economies and polities, instructing the population to change their behaviour, and restricting whole areas of economic activity. They might also have thought about the management of the pandemic and the ways in which the health services, big pharma, and national and local governments have administered their activities in these remarkable times. Many of those staring out the window could have easily concluded that they were critical of the management efforts of those to whom they looked for some sort of help. In the autumn of 2021 in the UK, 145,000 people had died due to Covid-19, and poor organization has something to do with that horrendous figure (House of Commons Parliamentary Committee Report, September 2021).

It became clear that the commissioning of the production and supply of PPE (personal protective equipment) was undertaken in very exceptional ways. MPs and Ministers – from one political party – were asked if they knew people who could be entrusted with the supply of such products and services, even if they and their companies had no previous experience of dealing with these pieces of equipment. The pandemic broke the rule book on government tendering procedures and as a result perhaps billions of pounds worth of business did not deliver on promises made and quality guarantees offered. Formal bureaucratic procedures were broken because it was accepted that bureaucracy was slow and painstaking and inefficient. And moreover, that formal control of these issues had belonged entirely to the European Union.

The tensions in the UK between an attenuated state bureaucracy, reduced in size and scope since 1980 (Jessop 2013), and the entrepreneurial zeal sought after by those committed to the market mechanism have created numerous problems over 2020–2021, not least of which are the number of dead citizens who were frail, or from minorities, or from deprived areas. The spread of the pandemic through care homes, where patients with Covid-19 were introduced as a way of increasing bed numbers available in NHS hospitals, remains another organizational scandal yet to be properly reviewed.

The state exists to manage and administer, yet its capacity to do so has been severely curtailed by the 50-year decline in centralized nationwide organization (Iedema 2003). The march of anti-bureaucratic forces, who see the state as a block to their profits and progress, is a story that is at the heart of Organization Theory in the post-WWII period (Thompson and Alvesson 2005; McSweeney 2006; Turner 2007; Argyriades 2010). However, we might assume that it is the state's responsibility to maintain public health even in the face of its declining ability to do so. Nothing else will! Entrepreneurialism (albeit another difficult term to define) is always a small-scale phenomenon (Jones 2014) and is incapable of delivering massive projects – such as sourcing PPE, developing track and trace techniques, and ensuring widespread vaccination – for health is not merely a market for the small number of the 'well off'. It is worth pointing out, however, that there are forms of indigenous entrepreneurialism across the world that do not represent an ideology of privatized greed but rather concern themselves with collective improvement, as we shall see a little later (Love 2018).

Yet, despite this widespread failure of private capital to supply societal needs in an emergency, there are those, and they are legion, who argue that the day of the organization is over. The zeal of the entrepreneur who is small scale, speedy, sinuous, specialized and sympathetic to market developments is held as the ideological way forward. These figures are seen as freeing the population from bureaucratic sclerosis. The many books praising Musk, Branson (2011), and Zuckerberg (see, however, Gillespie 2015; Boje and Smith 2016; Osland 2020) weigh down the shelves of airport book shops as if they are representative of a modern 'non-organized' (i.e. individualistic) way of doing things. But behind the individual mask of these entrepreneurs lie the many other faces (and bodies and minds and souls) that organize their enterprises with very traditional methods and procedures. Employees of many so-called entrepreneurs are locked into mega-corporations – whilst their leaders might pretend otherwise.

Why a Shift to Other Forms of Organizing Outside the Organization?

The answer to why there has been a noticeable move from studying 'organizations' to studying 'organizing' in non-organizational forms is a complex one. First, as we have already seen, is the attack upon bureaucracy from many places and from many scholars (Argyriades 2010). Whilst bureaucratic forms of organizing have been around for 5000 years (Mouzelis 2017; Wittfogel 1957; Albrow 1970) periodically they become subject to critique when they appear to ossify power in the hands of a priestly class of administrators rather than leaving it untouched in Royal and aristocratic palms. The fortunes of bureaucracy move with the times, oscillating between highly formal systems of administration like those that (supposedly) underpin representative democracies, to the personal, unpredictable interactions that underlie informally governed absolutism. In 2021, we live in a large wave of anti-bureaucratic sentiment partially brought about in the UK by critique of the EU's apparatus and partly in the USA by Trumpian attitudes to the Washington 'swamp'. These are merely newer versions of attack upon the post-war consensus around welfareism, a strong state, and legislative brakes upon unfettered libertarianism (Du Gay 2000, 2005).

Second, the theoretical move against bureaucracy undertaken by Popper and Hayek (Hayes 2008), for example, ushers in an interest in, and advocacy of, the notion of the 'market'. In many perspectives the market is seen as opposed to bureaucracy, and also as superior to it, because it supposedly delivers cheaper, more effective goods and services compared to a state bureaucracy. The Soviet Union is usually invoked at this point to tell stories of massive inefficiencies that socialism engendered and a concomitant failure to deliver the goods that the population wanted. As the 'market' apparently triumphed in the early 1990s, 'History' came to an end (Fukuyama 2006). In the discipline of Economics, 'Organization Theory' has come to be greatly influenced by Oliver Williamson (1993) whose work on information costs and the inefficiencies of bureaucracy in keeping these economic costs down provides another part of the context for 'organizations' to be seen as problematic (Rowlinson 1996: chapter 4). This places the market as superior to bureaucracy as a 'mode of organizing' because it is cheaper. As I write this, Boris Johnson is proclaiming to the Tory Party conference that fuel shortages across the UK are something that the market mechanism must put right and not a centralized government (although troops have been deployed to move fuel!).

Third, an ideological movement in the 1980s led by the Reagan and Thatcher administrations, emphasized the liberation of the energies of the people by encouraging them to become 'entrepreneurs'. Self-made women and self-made men were to populate the economy with the happy buzz of release from the shackles of long-term employment within a large corporation. The labour force was to noticeably shift in the Anglo-American world, throughout the 1980s and beyond, from work in very large organizations with employment numbers in the tens of thousands to massive numbers of tiny enterprises running with a handful of staff, often bound through marriage and parenthood (Jones 2014). These small-scale firms had little need for an understanding of full 'bureaucracy'. Where large firms continued to employ massive numbers, an associated notion of 'intrapreneurialism' (Jones 2014) was tried out in order to maximize the personally motivated drive that came from the unfettered release of pent-up creativity within the organization. Creativity was seen as a product of the breakdown of bureaucratic organization and not as its purpose. 'Creative destruction' (Schumpeter 1942) became an acceptable strategy at national and corporate levels (Ghoshal and Westney 1993).

Fourth, as we approached the twenty-first century, the entrepreneurial drive of staff, 'liberated' often by the widespread downsizing of firms throughout the 1990s due to the fad for Business Process Engineering and the like, took new forms (Case 1999; Prujit 1998). *The Apprentice* TV show encouraged young and self-absorbed people to set up new enterprises subordinate to large-scale business 'leaders' such as Alan Sugar and Donald Trump. Franchising of operations (Ozanne and Hunt 1971; Alon et al. 2020), outsourcing, subcontracting into smaller and smaller units, the gig economy (Duggan et al. 2020; Butler 2021), the rise of the precariat and so on, are all part of the move against bureaucracy and against the seemingly secure 'contract of employment', towards the temporary and one-off contract to supply services (Hecksher 1994). It would be a mistake to underestimate the importance of the contract of employment to Organization Theory (Freedland 2006). It underlies and ties together the spatial metaphor of the pyramid which is so essential to understanding many organizations. If everyone is an entrepreneur or even an intrapreneur, their contracts of employment are very likely to be non-existent or very vague. Their ties to the grouping from which they receive payment are based not on a predictable monthly salary but on a delayed payment of a receipt for services rendered. Nor can the entrepreneur claim sick pay or call upon company HR facilities in times of need (Dundon and Rafferty 2018). They have no insurance unless paid for separately by themselves. Their administrative costs are borne by themselves, not by the large organization for whom they may have once worked. The displacement of costs – out from the corporation and into the home or small workshop – was massive.

Fifth, the large organization usually required very large premises (Dale and Burrell 2003; Negri 2018; Ibrahim et al. 2021). Some of the largest buildings in Canary Wharf in London hold 7000 clerical and administrative staff (Harris 2015). These were built 30 years ago and have possibly reached the end of their utility for what they were designed. Large buildings require expensive 'facilities management' and have significant maintenance charges. Covid-19 has probably accelerated an already extant pressure to downsize the organization's HQ buildings. The consequence of this is the move into smaller, cheaper, rented (not owned) accommodation which is probably not as prestigious as a city centre site but is 'cost effective' and more flexible. It may also be easier to reach by the commuter. As the large edifices of the organization become abandoned, or turned into high rise flats, the bureaucracy itself becomes less visible. The corporate skyline loses its iconic skyscrapers to multiple occupants all sharing increasingly cheap concrete and glass. After 9/11 there was a corporate move out from central Manhattan to other boroughs of New York but this only hurried up a process already underway in 2001 (Chernick 2005).

Sixth, the organizing necessary to oppose the large corporation or the State may take a non-organizational form through digitalization. For example, in their call for papers on *Organizing Outside Organizations*, Czarniawska, Miscione, Raviola, da Silveira, and Tarim (2021) maintain that

> We have been studying formal organizations for at least a century, if not longer, and there is not much that we do not know about them. A recent phenomenon – the digital transformation of contemporary organizations – has also attracted much attention, and great many studies were done, with interesting results. But digitalization opened also wide doors to organizing outside, oftentimes in spite of, and against,

formal organizations. How do people organize demonstrations in Belarus, in Poland, or, for that matter, how do The Proud Boys do it in the USA?

Seventh, it has become almost common sense in commentaries about recent changes in the ways in which work in the West has become organized, to say that it's all about *platforms not pyramids*. This suggests that the use of ICT has replaced the need for tall bureaucratic structures by 'flat', 'open' systems to which access is quick and easy, and that workers (and employees more generally) live their daily lives organized via 'electronic envelopes' (Felstead et al. 2005) which they carry around with them (Felstead and Jewson 2002) in each and every one of their mobile excursions, including those in working time.

This seventh point, and all that has been listed previously, suggests that the day of 'organization' has gone. We shall come to understand that this is *not* the case. But first, we must consider how broad based a term 'organizing' actually is.

3   What Is Organizing?

Alexander Pope, like many close personal friends of monarchy, would have us believe that social order is paramount when he proclaimed that 'Order is Heaven's first law' (Alexander Pope, Essay on Man, Epistle iv). Organization and chaos are seen as irredeemably opposed (Burrell 2018). The ordering process is essential to stasis and yet brings into our view the time dimension associated with predictable change. Thus, once one starts to see the importance of metaphor (Morgan 1986: Oswick et al. 2002; Cornelisson et al. 2008), one immediately confronts the problem of how to build into the solid metaphor of a pyramidal 'organization', the major issues of *fluidity and change*. Structures such as a 'wall' or a 'boundary' to contain an organization and give it a necessary form, rigidity, and sense of protection, definitely interfere with process and movement, inwards and outwards, as the Berlin Wall came to symbolize so clearly. Binaries of an either/or kind are a key part of our thinking and, as we shall see, Organization Theory is beset by many of them. Here, the procedures whereby a line is drawn as a boundary between two elemental forces that govern organizing on one hand, and organizations on the other, is seen as a major way forward for some analysts. They place on one side a structure, and on the other is deemed to be a process. They place on one side organization, and the other is deemed to be 'organizing'. And this binary is to be found in many places (Langley and Tsoukas 2010; Nayak and Chia 2011) as a major defining framework within Organization Theory.

Structure is associated with stasis, rigidity, form, architecture, duration. It is about capturing and fixing what something looks like from within and without. Process is about fluidity, movement, change, metasisis, the short-lived. It is about movement and dynamism and flow. Theorists of organization have tended to focus upon the former, treating it as superordinate, as the many texts on 'organizational design' will testify (Daft et al. 2017) but the latter, the subordinate part of the binary, has become an interest for some.

DOI: 10.4324/9781003150503-3

For example, Haridimos Tsoukas and Robert Chia have utilized *Process Theory* in their approach to social and organizational change. Tsoukas and Chia say in *Organization Science* (2002) that patterns are emergent accomplishments and are always in a state of 'becoming'. In this, they follow Bergson and James whom they label as 'process theorists' and argue change precedes organization ontologically, and so organizations are always everywhere in a state of 'becoming' rather than just 'being'. Organization is thus a 'secondary accomplishment' to becoming (Hatch and Yanow 2003; Mills and Novicevic 2019). Their focus is upon micro-change at the level of the everyday and quotidian. They use a number of derived examples, including that classic case of jazz improvisation (Hatch and Cunliffe 2006; Hatch and Weick 1998) to show that organizing is constantly changing due to contingent and somewhat unpredictable factors. 'There is a world out there that causes the organization to respond but the pattern of response depends upon the organization's own self-understanding' (Tsoukas and Chia 2005, p. 578).

Karl Weick's *enactment theory* is seen by Tsoukas and Chia as offering an analysis of change but one set within social order, and as therefore understanding change less well than he might. However, one of Weick's achievements was in shifting attention away from complete concentration upon organizations to some aspects of organizing. 'Organizations are connected actions' opined Weick and Roberts (1993) as they grappled with change but someone who is committed to more structured approaches might point out that these connections are repeated and are to be found in organizational types and in recognizable categories. For Weick, in his *Social Psychology of Organizing*, enactment means that 'managers construct, rearrange, single out, and demolish many "objective" features of their surroundings. When people act they unrandomize variables, insert vestiges of orderliness, and literally create their own constraints' (Weick 1997, p. 243). Thus, people make sense of their own world. But the famous piece on the collapse of sensemaking in the Mann Gulch wildfire by Weick in *Making Sense of the Organization* (2001) is reviled by many firemen and women around the world because of its implications for action. Many firefighters see its conclusions as positively dangerous for their own survival because of its emphasis on one's own sensemaking and the breakdown of bureaucratic order (Basbøll 2010). Jacob Rees-Mogg, Leader of the UK House of Commons (November 5, 2019), adopted the same position when saying the residents of Grenfell Tower should have 'used their own common sense instead of following fire-brigade advice'. In embracing something akin to 'subjectivism' and by emphasizing the importance of process not structure, Weick threatens (literally as well as figuratively) those who believe in the objective powers of formal organization (Dwyer and Hardy 2016).

Practice based approaches to Organization Theory seek to show how everyday action is organized, looking at what is actually done at the micro level and at the subjectivist perceptions of practitioners (Nicolini 2009). Geiger and Antonacopoulou (2009) show that approaches which understand organizational practice in a non-cognitive, non-positivist, and non-rationalist ways enrich our understanding of organizational life – particularly in circumstances of breakdowns and conflicting ethical values. A Habermasian conception of practice is introduced which allows for discourses which are argumentative in nature. In other words, organizing is fraught with conflict and difference as well as the pursuit of order.

Turning to developments in ethnomethodology, Maynard and Clayman (1991) considered the ways in which ethnomethodology has developed and see this as extremely diverse, including for example, epistemic sociology, conversational analysis, discourse studies, and 'institutional analysis' (what ethnomethodologists tend, somewhat narrowly, to consider that Organization Theory represents to them). They do consider the ways in which the investigations into scientific practice in the organizational context, especially within the laboratory, have been informed by ethnomethodological interests. The discovery of 'pulsars' for example was shown by Garfinkel in 1981 to depend upon situated conversations and bodily practices. Lynch (1985) and Livingstone (1987) are also examples of carrying on the tradition of this work studying the cultures of biologists and mathematicians, respectively. Anne Rawls (2008) tried to bring the story up to date by considering Garfinkel's impact upon twenty-first-century work. For example, Heath and Luff (2000) considered the objections to the use of computers by medical consultants within hospitals to record notes because handwriting notes allowed them subtlety of expression and encoded terms that computerization would remove. For the computerized notes are not 'situation and sequence sensitive'. Rawls argues that video is an essential tool for the ethnomethodologists because it allows a record of the sequencing of ordering techniques to be observed and analysed with human interactions. This is a method suitable for the search for organizing in difficult situations rather than for fixed, formal, and everyday organization.

Because of his *The Interpretation of Cultures* (1973) Clifford Geertz has been held up by some as the most important theorist of *interpretive social science* since Max Weber (Abolafia et al. 2014). Influenced by Schutz's concept of the 'lifeworld', Geertz has concentrated upon the notion of culture and this has been taken up in the study of 'organizing' as a key concept from anthropology. He says (Geertz 1973, p. 5) 'I take culture to be those webs (of significance) and analysis of it to be therefore … an interpretive one in search of meaning'. Webs of significance are his focus and they are everywhere. However, the interpretivist must live with both confusion and incompleteness. This approach has been taken up by Stephen Barley (1983) and Linda Smircich and Marta Calas (1987) in their interpretive analyses of organizational culture where the term is taken to mean shared intersubjective meanings rather than a unitary monolith capable of being shifted by senior management via a tool kit (for example, by followers of Peters and Waterman (1982) and the consultancy industry). Methodologically, Geertz has influenced many contemporary writers in Organization Theory, where, for example, Jeffcutt (1994) looks at traditions of representation through Geertzian frames, as has Joanne Martin (2001) in her consideration of culture under postmodernism. This concentration upon semiotics and the phenomenological life-world marked Geertz and his followers within a process orientated Organization Theory, as very distinct from the functionalist orthodoxy (Linstead and Grafton-Small 1992).

Finally, in this type of process-based approach to organizing, Mikhail Bakhtin developed a polyphonic concept of truth wherein truth is not a statement, a sentence, or a phrase, as was assumed by certain Austrian philosophers within logical atomism. Rather, truth is a number of mutually addressed, yet contradictory and logically inconsistent, statements. There is no univocal truth, for many simultaneous voices make up the polyphonic truth. In *The Dialogic Imagination* (1975; Todorov 1984) Bakhtin develops the notion of 'heteroglossia' which establishes the importance of utterances being comprehensible only within a context: and contexts *differ*. Text always requires context for meaning to be generated. To make an utterance means to 'appropriate the words of others and populate them with one's own intention'. This creates an interpretivism where meaning is seen as being specific to particular interactions between particular individuals. Bakhtin's work has been used in organizational communication, and by those such as Czarniawska (1997) who seek to 'narrate the organization'. As we shall see later this concern for process and organizing has had some effect upon 'Indigenous Organization Studies' (Love 2018).

Whilst the term 'organization', then, tends to seek out the fixed, the firm, the regular, the predictable, the structured, the large scale, the bureaucratic, the grand edifice, the study of 'organizing' (rather than 'organization') has thrown up a major cleavage between Organization Theorists. Theorists of 'organizing' tend to seek out the changeable, the malleable, the irregular, the unexpected, the movement in process, the small scale, and the everyday accomplishment of order. Often this means they search out extreme work and unusual situations, even ambulance-chasing in some cases, such as that evident possibly in some of the research activities of Karl Weick. But this binary can only take us so far. Everyday life is both pre-organized for us and we organize it ourselves. We inhabit structure as bearers of it, carrying it around with us whether we are aware of it or not. But by acts of will, of sins of omission or commission, of failures and achievements, we humans also process the organizing of our worlds in and out of existence.

In the next chapter, we shall see how those interested in organization theory have dealt with the issues of process and structure, organization and organizing, stasis and movement, order and change.

4 What Is Organization Theory?

In social science, we are faced with the questions of what is our *explanandum* and what is our *explanans*. The former is that chosen by the analyst which is to be explained, the latter is that chosen by the researcher which is to do the job of explaining. It is my view that Organization Theory's *explanandum* concerns an interest in the study of 'organizations' by a concentration upon both 'organization' and in 'organizing'. It is concerned with theorizing about, analysing, and researching both the active verb sense of a process of organizing, and the fixed structural sense of the noun 'organization'. This also appears to parallel a rather clear binary between noun and verb, fixed and fluid, structure and process (Clegg et al. 1996; Fineman et al. 2009). However, one needs something more dialectical here, in which it is possible to take two apparently distinct and contradictory notions and synthesize them in such a way as to be beyond conflictual relations, heading towards something more constructive and progressive.

In seeking to escape from imprisonment by this binary, Karen Dale and myself began to argue that the 'riparian' metaphor for structure and process was a way forward (Burrell and Dale 2010, 2014). This is to conceptualize a way out of Organization Theory's conceptual predicament with binaries, by beginning with the simple notion of the river bank, which is normally seen as a solid containing fluidity. The process of the river is structured by the solid materiality of the banks. But we recognize the ways in which the process of the river's movement *interacts* with the solidity of the river's apparent boundaries. The bank of the river is in constant motion and its dynamic movement is, in fact, heavily structured. There is process and structure in both the river and in its banks. Therefore, 'organization' and 'organizing', whilst they may appear to be about structure and process in that order, are in fact *both* about structure and process. However, that dialectical solution is not to everyone's taste by any means. The *explanans* that have become the focus of the academic community's viewpoints are various and colourful

DOI: 10.4324/9781003150503-4

but often miss out on a dialectical vitality to engage with the subject matter, beyond adopting one side of the simple binary of either stasis and shiftings.

Throughout the history of Organization Theory, there has been one important binary concerning what constitutes the 'inside' and the 'outside' of the organization. Obviously, this leads to a question about what boundary we might place around the 'organization'. This was a *spatial* matter both of establishing an explanandum and creating disciplinary walls behind which our 'leaders' could establish control. Where was the boundary of the organization if people came to and fro every day into work? Is a ship isolated at sea a clear example of a bounded organization, or is it the Admiralty, or the War Ministry upon which one should focus? By the mid-1960s the question appeared to be, was the physical location of a factory or an office block that which marked out the organizational boundary? Was it the full-time list of employees as defined by Human Resources? Was it the legal reach of a corporate entity as defined within a national legal framework? Boundary drawing everywhere was in full flow. Each profession proffered its own line of demarcation. But this has consequences. The two dimensional and surface-based mapping of a field undertaken by researchers with their eye on the horizon, ignores that which lies submerged just between the rock formations, or is masked by the deep and dark liquidity (Bauman 1990) of the ongoing processes. There is a need for 3D thinking beyond superficial boundaries.

There has also been a question of the *temporal* origins of organizational forms. Rivers are often used as a process metaphor since the time of Heraclitus, so if we push the riparian metaphor, discussed earlier, a little further, it takes us to the possible origins of organizing and organizations along the banks of the great river valleys of the world. The Nile, Tigris–Euphrates, and Yangtse may all lay claim to great civilizations (Wittfogel 1957) to do with hydraulic control of river levels throughout the year, the prediction of the flood season through record keeping and astronomy, the use of good alluvial soil to produce an annual surplus, and the raising of large armies of workers to build and maintain flood defences. But why not the Amazon, the Niger, and the Mississippi? Well, perhaps the remnants of their past great civilizations still remain undiscovered by being wood-based cultures. There is certainly a case to be made that the flood defences and hydroelectric work in the Tennessee Valley undertaken in the 1930s and 40s produced much interest in the role the state could and should play in the New Deal and in associated industrial development (Selznick 2011; Smith 2006).

And if we push the attempted human control of large water systems beyond the river valley and out to the ocean, we must note that the lone ship at sea (Law 1984; Clegg 2017), for many centuries, represented the taking of your own specific culture with you, emplaced within the naval vessel. Here, on board the warship, we confront the transportation of a form of organizing the sailor recognizes. It carries domestic organization across the ocean to foreign parts. Thus, the actual chronological time at your home port, the location of home on a grid system of longitude and latitude, the ship's furniture and fittings, the culture of hierarchy and respect, drawn specifically from naval power, were all placed on board the vessel as part of its organization. Control at a distance also involves 'rum, sodomy, and the lash' as expressed in Churchill's offer of a precise organizational analysis of what he thought controlled sailors whilst at sea. This characterisation mattered because, at the time, he was First Secretary of the Admiralty. In any event, we need to remind ourselves of two things. Naval power carried with it much that was not planned nor managed, yet was very material. Tsing (2012, pp. 144–145) indicates that the Royal Navy unknowingly exported around the world the fungus of 'dry rot' which had originated solely in the high Himalayas without any human consequence. But once the tentacles of Empire embraced Himalayan timber for its ship repair yards, dry rot spread everywhere across the world where timber was used. Second, whilst we should understand that wherever humans seek to organize there will be grave unplanned consequences, we must note that most planning is concerned with controlling the ambient setting of work, often through great hardship and even violence.

In another example of the importance of the binary in conventional Organization Theory, the interest is often upon improvement of organizational life *as seen from the point of view of senior management*. Rarely is the perspective of the organizational member at the foot of the hierarchy adopted (Contu 2008; Ackroyd and Thompson 2016). It is assumed that principles are discernible by which all human life could be improved by better organization and improved management. And it is further assumed that stability, order, and economic progress will all be the incontrovertible tenets upon which 'betterness' and 'improvement' will be measured. Thus,

> Mary Follett devoted a lifetime to searching for the true principles of organization which would ensure a stable foundation for the steady, ordered progress of human well-being ... She realized that the principles which should determine organization are identical, no matter what the purpose which that organization is designed to serve.
>
> (Rowntree 1940, p. x)

Notice that Rowntree was writing about Follett (who had died in 1933) in the very early years of the Second World War. As we have seen, this period is often regarded as the essential beginnings of managerialism (Burnham 1941) – the idea that the day-to-day management of the state, the economy, and population are essential to bringing about military success and civic survival. And it is suggested that by the early 1940s all warring states are forcibly engaging in (relatively) full managerialism, for without this move, defeat is assured. There is a well-established argument that has been made on both sides of the Atlantic that Organization Theory begins to take off in this period and emerges from the conflict fully developed from about 1948. It is as old as the National Health Service and the North Atlantic Treaty Organization, two forms of organizing previously unobtainable in the 1930s.

This strand of Organization Theory is a very powerful one. It is about good organization designed by, and for, senior management cadres, essentially for military purposes wherein the state is the major client for all services within the wartime economy. At the time of the First World War, Max Weber (in Gerth and Mills 2014) wrote about the huge range of organizational forms of the military throughout history in order to find out what worked effectively (bureaucracy apparently) in bringing about military success. So, after WWII, non-bureaucratic forms of organizing in and around the state were seen for decades in the West as somewhat suspect. Much work was done from within and around this perspective, not least of which were those texts that sought to understand it only in order to *undermine* it. Today, there are those who seek to avidly defend bureaucracy, rationality, record keeping, and legitimacy as key elements of organizing human life – and as fundamental to a better quality of life for the population (Du Gay 2013). On the other hand, there are significant numbers of scholars who see the post-bureaucratic organization as much more important in understanding health, the productive economy, the state, and many forms of consumption (Reed 2011; Schofield 2001; Thompson and Alvesson 2005). This comparison has generated huge amounts of discussion (e.g. Argyriades 2010), all about to become even more heated in the post-pandemic circus of internal inquiries.

What is missing from this managerially inclined side of the binary is the view from the office and the shop floor. How might the working lives of subordinate members of the organization be improved? What would 'improvement' look like? Are well-being programmes, for example, really fit for purpose or do they make employees merely fit for senior management's purpose (Dale and Burrell 2015)? Is the process of the 'responsibilization' (Fleming 2017) of employees for their own health and well-being, which is now very well developed, in fact permissive of organizational derelictions of a duty of care? This raises the question (albeit much later on the agenda of most readers perhaps) of how might the lives of academics who study such issues be improved?

The Foundational Principles of Organization Theory – or Not?

This book rests upon the notions of the 'organization', 'organizing', and 'Organization Theory' being seen within a set of foundational principles (Tsoukas and Knudsen 2005). However, my perspective is not necessarily based upon the usually accepted disciplinary fundament. I wish here to contest the assumptions that many of my colleagues in Organization Theory would base their work upon.

The first area that should face contestation is the single assertion that the sole task of Organization Theory is to improve social and organizational practice so that management can develop human potential to solve problems as best as the species might. The working assumption here is that philosophical 'pragmatism' should be the basis upon which the effectiveness of thought in my area might be evaluated. Has it made a difference in human practice that can be measured and demonstrated? If it has, is it superior to those nostrums that are disconnected from measurable improvements? Often unquestioned within US thought (Morgan 2014), pragmatism has come to predominate the philosophical trappings of Organization Theory in many places, including in mainland Europe. It stands proud at the moment in practice theories of various kinds. But what are its weaknesses? Let us remember that other epistemologies and other ontologies are available (e.g. Irigaray 2008; Gaim and Clegg 2021).

The second of these foundational principles for any research programme is a necessary contestation of what constitutes good management of the discipline itself. There is a strong view, especially within the USA, that Organization Theory rests on the shoulders of giants and should respect and honour the work of all of who have gone before. This incrementalism is about a community respecting its forebears and seeking to show it has an honourable tradition of intellectual growth in the face of new theories, new empirical work, and new colleagues entering the profession. Arguments about things should not be allowed to develop too much, in case they problematize the very basis of the discipline. And the word 'discipline' is used here advisedly, to mean the power structure of the body of knowledge which decides – or seeks to decide – what is right and what is wrong and then what should happen to transgressors.

We are encouraged to be 'professional', to 'submit' our papers, and to not bring the field into disrepute. In other words, we are told how to behave and what is not permissible. And much of this is unchallenged within a field, for it is often what holds the field together. Norms, values, mores, and ethical standards – albeit of particular kinds – are the currency of the mainstream. My colleagues might correctly reject this view as disdainful of them, of course, pointing out their agency and choices in such matters. But often the constraints upon our work are invisible or seen only out of the corner of an eye in a meeting, or whispered in an ear by a senior, respected member of the faculty. We are captured by this normative mesh and subjected to disciplinary and socio-technological domination. Within this net we must accustomize ourselves, without reservation, to a willingness to accept command and embrace an illusion of freedom set within exploitation. In other words, within disciplinary boundaries, we ingrain a subjectivity that is willing to submit to control (Negri 2018, pp. 19–21). We do not normally, as normal scientists (Kuhn 1963), escape the norms that bind us. Perhaps, however, some wriggle room is possible within the iron cage of career.

Therefore, in this text, I will aim to present an overview of the theoretical and empirical work currently going on in the field of Organization Theory and to offer some critical comment on the state of knowledge in the discipline and suggest what might be done to ameliorate its shortcomings. To do this we must put Organization Theory into some sort of context. It is, of course, important to be fair minded and yet maintain a freshness in thinking about our topic. So, we cannot in all fairness neglect the orthodox work being done across parts of the world on how and why to organize our lives. But in the spirit of dialectics, we need also to consider the edgy, the marginal, the worrying, the harrowing, and the problematic in what we point to.

The third questionable assumption which follows from the second is the widely found political consensus that Organization Theory is a science and should model itself upon the natural sciences. Mathematical dexterity is to be prized with large data sets and sophisticated modelling, showing that Organization Theory can match the rest of economics and business analysis. Borrowing metaphors from the sciences becomes a way of allying oneself with high status elements of the scientific enterprise (Oswick et al. 2011; Reed and Burrell 2019). Many scientific fields such as chaos theory, quantum physics, and software development have been plundered for notions that are deemed worthy of importation and exploitation. In the UK and elsewhere the rise of the assumed importance of the STEM subjects (science, technology, engineering, and maths) has come to dominate thinking and a firm desire has been evinced, especially within organizational psychology, to be at high table in the tent and not hanging around outside in the cold waiting for a few crumbs. In this desire to be taken seriously, Organization Theory is held up by the founders as an 'administrative science' within very constraining boundaries (Donaldson 1988, 1998, 2003; Aldrich 1988). There are, however, alternative visions about knowledge production that need asserting.

Fourth, and by way of example, Michel Foucault argues that criticality is essential in the face of 'regimes of truth'. He attempts to foreground such a position when he says

> There are times in life when the question of knowing if one can think differently than one thinks, and perceive differently than one sees, is absolutely necessary if one is to go on looking and reflecting at all. In what does (activity) consist, if not in the endeavour to know how and to what extent it might be possible to think differently, instead of legitimating what is already known?
>
> (Foucault 1985, pp. 8–9)

From this, one gathers that one must interrogate the norms that constitute our discourse and our very subjectivity. To do this, the writer must be working within a discourse rather than standing outside it (Westwood and Linstead 2001; Grant et al. 2009). And they must expose the limits of extant knowledge by, *inter alia*, disrupting epistemological and ontological certainty. For regimes of truth determine what is possible to think, what can be said, and what must remain unsaid. A discipline must be open enough in order for us to challenge our prejudices and raise the possibility of the impossible. What the discipline considers is impossible must surely be a starting place for our thoughts at some point, if we value intellectual excitement at all (Clegg 1994; McKinley and Starkey 1998; Miller and Rose 2008).

Thus, imagine, please, a lecture hall that is 10 metres wide with a base wall of this distance. This wall represents the vast range of how humans have tried to organize their lives over the last 10,000 years. Almost all of what we are taught today about how to manage ourselves that is claimed to be sensible, realistic, possible, effective, and right-minded fits into the first 1 metre of that wall on the right-hand side. This small section is where the classic bureaucratic organizational form and the market are to be found. Nine metres stretching to the left of historical and spatial experimentation, of repeated trial and effort, long-lasting sustainability, short-term expediency, and constant living with existential crisis are undiscussed, unspoken of, invisible, unimagined. It is said to be madness to contemplate these 9 metres of possibility in 2022. What we have been proffered as 'sensible' in organizing our lives and the lives of others is thoroughly Panglossian; it is 'for the best in the best of all possible worlds'. Right thinking by thoughtful, good-intentioned human beings has got us to where we are in the organizations and the organizing of our world through, for example, markets and digital networks. There are no alternatives worth contemplating. So, says this regime of truth, just get on with it. However, seeing the world from the top table often makes one oblivious to deep history. Today's problems are just too pressing for the empowered. They live from crisis to crisis. Well, in part, and encouraged by Foucault, this book is going to take a small step to move outside the comfort zone of conventional Organization Theory and contemplate the unthinkable by looking, later, to sketching the left-hand side of the wall.

The writing upon the 9 metres of our wall contains a panoply of organizational forms found across history but it is by no means an exhaustive one. For much of these experimental and long-lived examples of organizing human life are not part of recorded history. They will have been in fabled legend in the oral histories that all societies possess, of course, but for 'advanced cultures' these approaches are seen as myths unworthy of historical merit. The writers within bureaucracies have already sifted out what they regard as unimportant and immaterial before quill touches parchment or stylus touches clay tablet. So matriarchal tribes, anarchist communes, a-cephalous groupings, riots and rebellions, social movements, warrior clans such as the Spartans, worker takeovers, machismo, the Mafia, Blat and quang-xi, nomadic peoples, Ubuntu, cooperatives, syndicalist forms of work, guilds, the farm, the village, the high-rise housing development, the hamlet, the family, the Household, the garden village, the naval vessel, and the most under-considered of all organizational forms – the slave plantation (Cooke 2003) – are forms of organizing hidden away in the fringes of Organization Theory. Many of these forms may be anathema to the reader but human beings have lived by them across the centuries. And lots more besides have fallen at the hurdle of not possessing a means of recording their exploits and achievements that did not solely involve human memory, or more materially, felled wood that rotted away.

These two structural components of our writing – the conventional, often militaristically based 1 metre and the unconventional, less violent 9 metres of our wall – will seek in part to carry the weight of *Organization Theory: A Research Overview*.

The fifth necessary contestation is the widely held view that the institutional 'leaders' of the discipline know what is best for the overall development of the field. Thomas Kuhn (1963) once argued that only with the decline and death of the leaders of particular fields of scientific knowledge would rapid, indeed revolutionary, progress come. And this is a belief held here too. Where are the off-piste ideas to come from if not the young and marginalized? In other words, those at the periphery and not the centre of the discipline should be listened to much more widely than they are. This small book will seek to allow space for these sorts of voices.

Thus, in the face of these five questionable elements about what is right and proper for Organization Theory, this book adopts the position that we should not be 'disciplined' into giving up critique of what went before. Indeed, it is our permanent duty to critique the field from within. Contestation is a sign of a healthy body of knowledge full of energy and movement (March 2005; Reed and Burrell 2019). Nor should it be questionable to start from a position that Organization Theory is, first and foremost, a part of the humanities and social studies, and we should set out from that assumption. Nor should the tenets of pragmatism – to value something by what 'impact' an idea has upon practice – be accepted as our measure of success. Other philosophical positions are also available. And finally, we are not going to slavishly follow the self-appointed leaders of the field who control the professional associations and the journals. It might even be a relief to many in the subject area to end what passes for 'leadership' of the discipline, so that unconstrained 'followership' might flower and become much more assertive and vibrant.

Consider the case of the American Academy of Management's reaction to the Presidency of Donald Trump and his attempt to prevent immigration from countries in which the Islamic religion was predominant (McGahan 2019). The Academy's espoused view was that it was a non-political organization and would hold no position on such issues of Presidential action, even though its membership may be fundamentally affected. Of course, it might be pointed out that to claim one is 'non-political' is a political statement in its own right and there was some limited debate in the journals about this. The outcome was that the officers of the Academy refused to behave in ways which they perceived to be 'un-safe'. And given the numbers of pro-Trump supporters across the USA, it was easy to assume some of them were part of the membership of the American Academy of Management. It was obviously much safer not to challenge the status quo, not to irritate pro-Trump supporters in the Academy, not to agitate against a sitting President, even though his anti-intellectualism was evident to most, and not to invite the unarmed and armed responses of MAGA supporters more widely. These are understandable motivations of personal safety but they do not necessarily make for ethical decisions of vibrancy and assertiveness.

Given all of this concern that I am raising here, and if there is so much contestation of Organization Theory's principles to be initiated, does this not suggest that we need to be organized – but differently? Let us begin by contesting the self-evident dominance of 'institutional theory'.

The Choke of Institutional Theory

There is a clear dominance in Western Organization Theory of 'institutional theory' in which, particularly in the USA, the field seems to have found a 'paradigm' in the classical Kuhnian sense (Reed and Burrell 2019). Indeed, one might guess that in the 2022 Research Excellence Framework evaluation in the UK, work using institutional theory will show a huge growth in influencing the writings of Business School academics. Why might this be?

First, there is a worrying move away from European-led approaches to theorizing the organizational world towards US-based ones (Thomas and Davies 2005). Critical Realism (Ackroyd and Fleetwood 2005; Fairclough 2005; Reed 2010; Ackroyd 2010), for example, which originates on this side of the ocean is virtually ignored in the USA. What is done in American social science has always played a role in influencing UK academic activity within the social sciences, of course, but what we now see is a willing and full embrace of such work when previously the influence of European social theory had ensured that not such a very strong hold could be exercised from across the Atlantic. This is partly Brexit related perhaps, and partly due to government-orientated commitment to STEM subjects where US dominance of science and technology is very widely accepted. We are expected by our league table obsessed managers to be dedicated followers of American fashion.

Second, institutional theory is a very 'safe' form of Organization Theory. Organization Theory that is 'safe' deals with topics and themes that consumers of the knowledge produced within its rubric find useful but ultimately unchallenging of perceptions. It may undermine conventional understandings by offering different interpretations of the success or failure of certain organizational moves and structures but it does not offer a threat to the existence of *underlying* structures of power, domination, and influence. These structures it accepts as a given, as almost immutable, and recognizes that challenges to the status quo need to be cast as improvements at the margin rather than as fully formed questioning of an existential nature. Thus, Organization Theory that is 'safe' should *not* be regarded as against change within organizational and managerial life. Its *raison d'etre* is to analyse the present day and the widely accepted, and suggest improvements if evidence for amelioration in these accessible ways arise from the research. Organization Theory of this ilk is not 'conservative' in terms of the everyday, the quotidian, the ways in which people live their organizational lives in some significant ways. It is only *fundamentally* conservative. For it stops, safely, at the point where it begins to question the very nature of organized life, the existence of managerialism, and the relevance of capitalism itself (Powell and Di Maggio 2012).

Everywhere one looks, in journals and in conferences, institutional approaches predominate numerically. One has to explain this phenomenon carefully (Scott 2005, 2008). Third, then, the approach is notoriously difficult to pin down. There is old institutional theory and new institutional theory, marked out very problematically with boundaries that make little sense (Greenwood and Hinings 1996). Jennings and Greenwood (2003, p. 195) contrast 'new institutionalism' and 'old institutionalism' when they say the old approach is to look at the structurally inert, to portray bureaucratization as inexorable and as representing an 'iron cage', and that the wider societal context of how far rationalization can develop given historical and cultural constraints is deemed to be very important. New institutionalism, on the other hand, is seen by Jennings and Greenwood to be more compelling. For it points to fields and networks of actors (especially, though not exclusively, organizations) as the locus of action. And it connects these fields with macro-societal processes *and* with micro-level interactions between actors (Scott et al. 1994). The 'and' is italicized in their own paper. As Adler et al (2014) has pointed out, whether new institutional theory manages to attain any real understanding of 'agency' is open to question, for historical and structural determinism pushes organizations towards an 'isomorphism' of their structures and processes, rendering actors much less agentic than one might imagine (Dacin et al. 2002). Knights (2009) argues that whilst power was always crucial in old institutional theory (even though it was often expressed as 'legitimate authority'), new institutionalism tends to neglect power and its complexity in the face of the desire to understand legitimacy and the persuasive mobilization of 'stakeholders' (Clegg 2010).

Fourth, it is a portmanteau term allowing all sorts of baggage to be carried along inside it (Scott 1987; Di Maggio and Powell 1991, p. 1; Palmer et al. 2008). This has the advantage of allowing a breadth of approaches to take shelter under a covering umbrella term, but it does render comprehending the overall picture as very tiring, confusing, and troublesome. Zucker (1987, p. 83, borrowing from Hughes in 1936) claims that 'the only idea common to all usages of the term "institution" is that of some sort of establishment of relative permanence of a distinctly social sort'. As Di Maggio and Powell point out, this can mean a handshake as well as very large-scale phenomena. Such a definition, with almost a cosmic range of interpretation, might not be seen as precise enough for many analysts. But precision is often disregarded if one is 'institutionalizing' a field oneself. The imperialist urge within institutional theory to colonize the field quickly has meant that it has utilized some blunt-edged weapons to be used by all its agents, wherever they find themselves in the field.

Fifth, it relates back to the history of Organization Theory, based as it is upon the interest in bureaucracy and bureaucratization (Thompson and Alvesson 2005). This encourages the idea that institutional theory is somehow originary to the project of theorizing about organizations. And given 'real' roots, it can claim a higher status for ideas than new entrants into the market. The status of ideas and their historical provenance is worryingly important to some scholars, despite their protestations sometimes about the importance of dealing with what is 'new'.

Sixth, it problematizes the issue of change around and about organizations which is a twenty-first-century question of huge importance (Dacin et al. 2002). It appears to embrace the problem of explaining enormous shifts in organizational life such as organizational death, merger, and acquisition and abuts to the field of strategic management in how to survive and prosper within highly competitive environments. But it says little about the consideration of the 'nature' of change itself, preferring to look at economic performance before and after major change programmes. Change is seen as shifts in structure over time rather than 'process'. In other words, conceptually and meta-theoretically, change is seen as episodic, with discrete beginnings and endings rather than as ongoing and processual over long time durations. Institutional theory appears to be about organizations, rather than organizing.

Seventh, because of its open generality in a meta-theoretical sense and its lack of self-reflection and discussion of questions of epistemology and ontology, it is remarkably capable of being incorporated by other theoretical perspectives, such as practice theory (Nicolini 2013). The danger, of course, is that the incorporator becomes the incorporated and that institutional theory's imperialist urges become satiated by bringing in many disparate areas under the umbrella, willingly or not. Institutional theory thus, over time, becomes less of a resource for the use of others but more akin to an ideational parasite, using others as its resource. This will be seen, perhaps, as disrespectful to many of my colleagues in the field but once one becomes part of a machinic consciousness, such as that now evinced by institutional theory, those outside the conceptual framework are honour bound to point out its limitations. It is part of a duty to initiate and continue critique.

So then, what of other strands of thought beyond institutional theory?

The Visible and the Invisible in Organization Theory

Rick Vogel (2012) in his piece for *Organization Studies* entitled 'The Visible Colleges of Management and Organization Studies: A Bibliometric Analysis of Academic Journals' looks at the articles within seven leading journals in the field over the last three decades. He performs an analysis of the topics covered over this 30-year period using bibliometrics and 'network visualisation'. He begins by saying that some people in Management and Organization Studies (MOS) can easily define themselves today as 'institutionalists, postmodernists and symbolists' but others are likely to be unaware of their intellectual home. Here, at the outset of his article, we have three nominations for contemporary fault lines in Organization Theory as evinced in the pages of AMJ, AMR, ASQ, JMS, Organization, Organization Studies, and Organizational Science. But he wishes to look at three periods, each of a decade, to identify shifts in intellectual concern in these 'leading' journals. Of course, his own analysis is already over a decade old.

In the decade of the 1980s, the predominant cluster identified by Vogel is contingency theory (Hickson et al. 1974). This dominated the field but in second place with much less centrality was 'resource and power dependency theory' (Pfeffer and Salancik 2003). Also identifiable as being of influence were behavioural theory (March 2005) and organizational symbolism (Peters and Waterman 1982).

In the 1990s, MOS diversified according to Vogel. He says (2012, p. 1027) 'Strikingly, contingency theory which dominated the field in the 1980s, can no longer be charted, even amongst the' periphery. Only behavioural theory maintained its core position. The main approach across the field became Interorganizational Relations (Powell, Van de Ven, and Poole 1995) but there is also a recognisable cluster around paradigm wars (Burrell and Morgan 2017).

In the 2000s New Institutionalism (Di Maggio and Powell 1991) has moved from the periphery of the field into the centre ground as identified in the frequency of publication in the seven journals. Interorganizational Networks, Behavioural Theory, and Paradigm Wars have all moved from the centre to the periphery. They have also been replaced by 'the Competence Perspective' which arose from the knowledge movement (Spender 1996; Foss 2007).

According to Vogel, over the three decades some approaches have shown some resilience. Organizational Symbolism and Behavioural Theory have lasted over this 30-year period. Only a few approaches survive longer than a decade and 'mortality' is particularly high at the periphery (Vogel 2012, p. 1033).

We can see through this bibliometric analysis that Organization Theory was a huge enterprise a decade ago. Today, it continues to cover very many areas and very many conceptual frameworks (Cunliffe 2008). In the face of this multiplicity, it appears to me that we need some freshness of thinking and perhaps some new agendas. Organization Theory appears to me to be tired and sluggish. My suggestion of a new direction for my discipline is to offer up a new explanandum – that which must be explained – of *organizational camouflage.*

This is both suggestive of a new theoretical object to explore in-depth *and* of the possible role of camouflage in explaining why organizations appear to be losing their saliency through their apparent disappearance. Surface and substrate, organization and context, have become obscured for reasons that turn out to be both rational and highly profitable. And here, the murkier the boundary between the two can be presented, the better it is for many senior corporate executives in both the private and public sectors. The next chapter will discuss the process of camouflaging organizations in a little more detail.

5   The Age of Camouflage

My integrative theme within this chapter for looking at current research in the field will be managerial 'camouflage' and its understanding as key to the modern organizational world. But first (and in keeping with the wider task) let me clear away some likely confusions. Andre Spicer (2017) has pointed out that there is much to see and reflect upon that is 'Business Bullshit' by which organizations thrive, through creating it, articulating it, and then consuming it. But this outpouring of non-sensical, contradictory rhetoric that means nothing, may reflect the related process of being employed within 'bullshit jobs' (Graeber 2014) which are seen by those that undertake them as 'utterly meaningless, contributing nothing to the world and should not exist'. Whilst this focus upon 'business bullshit' and 'bullshit jobs' is to be welcomed as informative, they are not constituent of what I regard as camouflage per se. It is the masking of processes and structures upon which I will concentrate, rather than their vacuity, for this is *the* significant activity. Because, as will be revealed, much camouflage hides from our view the continued importance of 'organization'. It is an optocentric search, of course, in that *looking* for the visible and invisible becomes crucial. But smelling a rat is also useful as a tool. In seeking out elements for the analysis of camouflage it is as well to note that this requires 'new' and challenging methods and ethics – for *how can you research something that is meant to be hidden by other human agents*? Embracing this particular contradiction will not be easy and it will require the skills more of an investigative journalist than an ethics-bound social science researcher (Sims 1991; McLeod et al. 2016; Buchanan and Bryman 2009). *The New Corporation* is a movie by Abbott and Bakan (2020) on corporate social responsibility (CSR) which has precisely this critical edge. By using talking heads and unofficial clips of CEO's revealing their real strategies it shows that organizations employing CSR 'have mounted a major charm offensive, rebranding themselves and rebranding the entire capitalist system as

DOI: 10.4324/9781003150503-5

having changed'. For 'major charm offensive' read the pursuit of maximum confusion in image and activity.

What the current situation starts to look like is the retreat of the predominant bureaucratic form of organization, associated with pyramidal structures in high profile locations and a certain showiness in marketing techniques, to positions hidden, as best as possible, behind 'camouflage'. The OED tells us that the word comes from the old French to disguise and deceive, possibly from 'camouflet', a whiff of smoke in the face. The connection between this origin and the phrase used to understand the *legerdemain* of conjurors – 'smoke and mirrors' – is notable. Camouflage, of course, is usually seen as a military term whereby the defensive, and more importantly offensive, capabilities of an organization are hidden. It requires the skills of painters and decorators who seek to mask what lies behind the netting, covering the real potentialities of the force at work. In the Falklands War, Argentine camouflage experts painted the runway at Stanley with what were apparently deep bomb craters, convincing the RAF that their attack upon the field by Vulcan bombers had been a success (Freedman 1982). It had not been, and Argentine aircraft continued to use the base throughout the conflict. In like vein, the painting over the cracks in the twenty-first century which has masked corporate power has been achieved behind a rhetoric of outsourcing and other forms of economic distancing. As we have seen, in place of familiar large organizational forms there has been pushed forward the notion of the small dynamic entrepreneur. More 'agile', less 'sclerotic' – allegedly – than the corporation, the small firm has been popularized for the opportunities to the owner, and the flexibility to the client, it offers. But it is the small entrepreneur who is the (stereo)typical case for intense scrutiny by State Income Tax authorities (Blackburn et al. 2005). Not only are the one-person hairdresser, plumber, and electrician easy targets for the Her Majesty's Revenue and Customs (Blackburn et al. 2005) and their equivalents worldwide, but so too are many SMEs. They are much less able to resist demands for more tax than are large corporations with whole departments devoted to tax avoidance. It is said that when the British Tax Revenue service sought to investigate the owner of one retail empire, there were presented with three pantechnicon's worth of documents; one holding paperwork in English, one in French, and one in Arabic. Faced with this mountain which would have taken all of the resources of HMRC years to digest, HMRC closed the case and accepted a very small cash settlement in the stead of a full investigation proceeding.

Nevertheless, the organizational advantages of using the small-scale entrepreneur who may be able to more easily shift activities quickly have become recognized and utilized by large corporations and the state. The latent (some might say manifest) function of this is that the large organization has, out front in their vanguard, a fleet of small-scale producers, maintenance workers, and service personnel for whom they have no responsibilities but over which they have *de facto* huge control. Complaints about service and products are thus directed to the outsourced activities, often from an outsourced complaints department. The classic tension between power and responsibility is expressed so clearly here. Large corporations which utilize camouflage lose responsibility but retain power.

What other functions of occlusion might the large organization seek? I have suggested in the paragraph above that the small-scale entrepreneur may well be seen to act as a mercenary, offering up his or her life on the front line for money and resources. They also offer a first target for the 'enemy' which we might proffer on some occasions is perceived to be the state in the form of the Inland Revenue; on others it may be to face direct customer dissatisfaction; in yet other cases it may be competitor interest that they deflect; in others, it may be consumer preferences for which they have responsibility. Small enterprises thus act as a protective shield for those that they have apparently replaced. Moreover, knowledge of an industrial or commercial sector is a very important asset and the corporation today is able to mask many details behind 'market' mechanisms, ostensibly held by other organizations, which are much more likely to be deemed as sensitive.

If one looks at camouflaging as a set of techniques, it often involves blurring the boundaries between entities so that they virtually disappear. The dazzle ships of the First World War (Dale and Burrell 2003) were painted so as to confuse the enemy observer about what shape the object had, what speed it was moving at, and in what direction it was heading. These are all techniques that the modern organization may well use in dealing with observers who may not be sympathetic. In an age of camouflage, and seeking to fuse both organization and organizing, one might suggest it is *shape, speed, and direction* which should be the vectors that organization theorists seek to analyse in all their objects of study (were we only able to perceive them).

Bob Cooper had the insightful notion that whilst Organization Theory should be interested in the 'Division of Labour' it should also concern itself in the 'Labour of Division' (Cooper 1990). The social sciences, he believed, progressed (or not) by their attention to making 'di-visions' in their subject matter. They make cuts in what they look at and by this slicing motion separate out what is interesting and what is not; what is central and what is not; what is to be explained and what is not. The di-vision typically offers two things to look at; the superordinate and the subordinate elements. We might imagine that camouflage seeks to render the subordinate superior to the superordinate. It allows that which it is not to stand in the stead of that which it is. Di-vision is a necessary and deliberate concomitant of camouflage. It encourages substitution of the one for the other (McCusker 1999; Schmidt 1979). The speeding destroyer at sea looks like a cloud formation because the labour of di-vision by the enemy observer is one leading to their disruption of perceptions deliberately planned by the camouflage expert. The latter's labour of di-vision in cloaking the enterprise, in effect is to mask by separation and thence create boundary confusion and failure to identify correctly. And so it is, today, in many organizational activities.

Look at branding for example. What began by referring to a specific mark upon an animal, human, or product made by a hot iron has become confused with organizational ownership. What students often fail to recognize is that the brand is no longer a mark of ownership – it is a signal to the market that hides ownership behind a label (Abbott and Bakan 2020). What branding often obscures is the key part of organizing that Organization Theory is interested in, that is to say power and its impact. What marketing all too often concentrates upon is the signalling device of the product rather than that which it obscures – ownership and control. Branding confuses these issues in a clear example of camouflage. In October 2021, Facebook, Messenger, Instagram, WhatsApp, Mapillary, and Oculus were brands that all had a six-hour outage caused by a 'Border Gateway Protocol' withdrawal. It came as a surprise to many to find that these were all part of the same corporation, hidden behind separate brands, but controlled centrally by Facebook (Taylor 2021). Only in instances such as this, when the shields are down, does the general public see the proprietorial interconnections that are masked by separate branding. And because of the bad publicity associated with the attention Facebook was receiving, on October 26, 2021 the company changed its name to 'Meta' (Guardian newspaper; October 27th, 2021). At a stroke of camouflage, its difficulties may just have eased, at least temporarily.

It is also the case at this juncture that we should point out that aesthetics (Strati 1999), often key to marketing interest in the generation of appearance and rendering something beautiful, always and everywhere carries with it some form of anaetheticization (Dale and Burrell 2003). This is a necessary parallel process of stripping beauty out, of deadening the senses, of facing the ugliness that might be found everywhere in production processes, especially for the workers involved in hard manual labour sourcing raw materials, or in those that service the cosmeticization of the product through spit and polish. We lose sight of what aesthetics has to offer by its deliberate 'stunning' nature and forget that which it is masking. It makes our range of senses dim and diminished when faced with the bright lights and new messages of some sorts of obscuring camouflage. The exquisite marble sculptures of the Renaissance required the sweat and even the deaths of many Italian quarry workers, for example. Many a museum across the world sports fine objects made of Italian marble which is the substance from which Michelangelo's 'Pieta' and the statue of George Washington is hewn. But often forgotten is that the quarrymen of Carrara, from where the marble was sourced, were nearly all fugitives from justice because no one else would work in those appalling conditions of dust and heavy lifting. The state was anaesthetized to their existence in the quarries of Carrara. The quarry later became a centre of anarchism and the advocacy of anti-state violence in the late nineteenth century. The ugly is masked by the beautiful. And this layering of cosmetics too, is a form of camouflage.

So, when we are told (Powell and DiMaggio 2012), that attention should be paid less to organizations themselves and more to the interstices between organizations where 'networks' thrive, supply 'chains' exist, 'subcontracting', 'offshoring', and 'outsourcing' occurs, and the 'franchise' predominates within 'the gig economy' populated by the 'precariat', it may be that these are, in some senses only forms of smokescreen, rendering the corporate world less visible. All of these problematize the 'organization', it is said, because the concept is so partial in its range of coverage. What I am suggesting here is that, in many cases, the concept of 'organization' now lies occluded by a thin film of masking tape.

Whilst the pyramidal, paper-based structure of the organization appears to have been superseded by platforms (and networks) reliant upon electronic, mobile communications, close analysis of the typical ICT network shows that above each platform rests a pyramid of control and strategic thought. But for those embracing the flatness of their new system parameters, with their eyes fixed firmly upon the horizon of individual success, the pyramid lies hidden in the clouds of obscurantism. And deliberately so.

Today, when many commentators see the *unbounded organization* with its outsourcing, the gig economy, franchising (Callaci 2021; Hoy et al. 2017; Rometch and Sydow 2006), self-employment, anti-bureaucratic moves everywhere to embrace entrepreneurship, and the liberation of individual potential in the market, they appear to accept that all such processes undermine the centralized corporation. Importantly, these are part of wider shifts in the sphere of what one might call *narcissistic individualism*. In the twenty-first century there have been marked changes in forms of social identity (Collinson 2003), the rise of possessive individualism (Macpherson 2010), of consumerism, and in selling the 'self' (Gergen 1991; Tseelon 1992; Davies 2015). All of these interrelated processes lead to the 'presentation of self' (Goffman 1972, 1992) and 'impression management' (Tedeschi 2013; Giacalone and Rosenfeld 2013) in the world of human capital (Spender and Marr 2005; Dubos 2017; Livingstone 1999; Fleming 2017) and to 'taking responsibility for your own career' (Livingstone 1999; Fleming and Sturdy 2009). But what is management for, if everyone manages themselves? Can the organization exist in such an individualized landscape of selves (Davies 2015; De Armitt 2013)? What is the lone entrepreneur and indeed 'entrepreneurship' good for (Jones 2014)? Reality and ideology are somewhat different and despite the range of anti-managerial texts that periodically sprout from the fertile ground of right-wing thinking in which the driven entrepreneur, motivated by profit, can solve all problems, there remains a huge managerial cadre across many societies. Managing organizations and the labour of others is still required, even in a clamouring landscape of individuals.

The organization has been transcended, allegedly, by a move outside its *boundaries*. But the old problem remains of the boundary between the inside and the outside of that which we seek to analyse (Latour 1996; Law and Hassard 1999; Latour 2017). Cooper (Spoelstra 2005; Hassard et al. 2007) used to say that the 'outside' is in fact the 'inside' because as in we humans, for example, the gut is actually the outside brought into our bodies, into us. Indeed, as we take breast milk from our mothers, the outside is immediately changed into the inside. Our gut is actually a part of the outside we think is inside us. It is not inside us. We, more accurately, are inside it. The organizational boundary reflects this philosophical problem of interiority/exteriority which experts, trained for example in the law, can use for camouflage to great effect.

Once we accept that this key conceptual boundary of 'bodies' is problematic we start to see the entanglement of the world (Barad 2003, 2007; Dale and Latham 2015). In this world of *materiality*, boundaries start to be even more problematic. What is thought superordinate becomes subordinate. Trees in forests become both influences and influencers of a microbial undersoil world. Fungi and lichen carry messages between plants in the Wood Wide Web (MacFarlane 2016). They live symbiotically with trees and plants who share common entanglements hidden in the sub-soil world. Using the notion of *entanglement* has proved to be a boon for Organization Theory as it both releases material objects from their passivity in most forms of the discipline and suggests that here, hidden from view under the forest floor, is a universe of complexity and cooperation of which we can only dream. The organization in the twenty-first century is part of the material and underground matrix which only appears, rhizomatically, (Deleuze and Guatarri 1974; Bogue 2008; Linstead and Thanem 2007) from time to time. It is camouflaged under a thin layer of humus.

Part of the task for a new, refreshed Organization Theory then, is to seek out both deliberate camouflage and the hidden entanglements enabling the invisibility of many organizations of which we are currently unaware. Let me produce a quote from Yiannis Gabriel (2019) which sums up some of the issues very well:

Our own institutions, the journals and conferences we follow, turn increasingly away from organizations to other subject matters … many scholars are turning away from the study of organizations even as they purport to make their home in it.

The issue for me is whether the apparent non-organizational foci of this work has occurred *either* because people have been fooled by the camouflage of the organizational world *or* because they see how organizing has transmogrified on the surface and that we need to understand this too. Undoubtedly for some highly respected scholars, the move away from the 'organization' as a key concept has to be seen, perhaps, as them falling prey to the art of camouflage. And perhaps within institutional theory, the recent extension of interest into interstices between institutional forms reflects such a fall too.

The argument in the rest of this book is that 'organizations' remain central to what we see around us. Or, more accurately, do *not* see around us. The 'market' is a gross portmanteau concept, everywhere anthropomorphosized to suggest 'it' has agency rather than the organized groups who manipulate it (McFall and Ossenden 2014; Rowlinson 1998). Just because organizations in 2022 hide for tax purposes, move out into smaller decentralized premises away from city centre locations, hide behind 'app' technologies, and disassociate themselves from the realities of overseas production in order to maintain ethical 'purity', this does not mean they have lost their saliency. Organization Theory may no longer be able so easily to view its objects of study as it once did, but with new methods, new concepts, and a new resolve to be investigative in a pointed way, it does have a future.

With this acceptance of the problems offered to Organization Theory by changing circumstances, it allows us to address Gabriel's deep concerns about 'our' future:

The implication is that the demise of organization studies is due to its own failures, especially its failure to adapt to different social and political realities. This critic might agree with Bruno Latour's (2004) diagnosis that critical thinking has run out of steam because it has attacked old familiar targets in old familiar ways with decreasing effectiveness.

(Gabriel 2020)

Taking this on board, this is a book partly about attempting to find new targets, new methods of approaching them sneakily, and of hitting them fairly and squarely (Steffy and Grimes 1986). But this is not for everyone. Some analysts are no doubt happy to accept that we live in an age of camouflage and carry on regardless. Some seek to investigate 'surveillance capitalism' (Zuboff 2019; Ball and McLeod 2014) which appears to observe our movements and preferences and peccadillos for its own purposes but seeks *not* to reveal itself to us. Why should we be interested in those large corporations who rationalize what they do as merely analysing our worthless 'data exhaust'? Perhaps surveillance techniques might be inverted to offer analyses subjecting agentic capitalism to intense, hidden observation. Perhaps alternative algorithms are available, or will become available, by which to escape the clouds of blinding exhaust from these intrusive companies which masks their purposes – and often their very existence. Intrusiveness and invisibility are interesting bedfellows (McNally 2011).

In the absence of such alternative algorithms, we might ask 'What has investigative journalism to offer'? This raises all sorts of questions about ethics and what is acceptable in terms of research. I once attended a seminar in which a colleague from another university claimed that his former role as an investigative reporter had shaped his research techniques and his primary objectives were to reveal the venality of the powerful and wealthy. His injunction to 'get the bastards – by any means possible' caused a ruction in the seminar room as those who thought that research ethics should never allow 'phone tapping nor rifling through wastepaper bins nor pretending to be something one was not, showed their horror. These opponents of the 'unmasking strategy by any means possible' won the day and across all disciplines, from the sciences to the social sciences and into the humanities, such techniques within investigative journalism are supposedly banned from 'science'. This begs the question of 'for whom is knowledge now ethical'? The protection offered by ethics is distributed asymmetrically.

In the British context then, the social science researcher is very much curtailed in what they are capable of doing by the spread of the science- and medicine-based codes of ethics (Komic et al. 2015). Permission has to be granted by subjects before they are able to be questioned or implicated in research activity. This sounds more than reasonable, but if one is seeking information from subjects who have clear and obvious reasons not to reveal their beliefs and activities to the researcher for financial or political reasons (amongst others), then social science is the poorer for it. What I am advocating here is a move out from the confines of the notion of a universal code of ethics for undertaking social science research, and the embracing of covert activity with some subjects of interest, usually the powerful and relatively invisible (Van Meijl 2000). We might label this approach *paraethics*.

A Programme of Research for Studying Organizational Camouflage

This envisaged programme of research using 'paraethics' (not anti-ethics, should it be of concern; see Bruce 2000) would ask a number of related questions.

- What are the techniques-in-use for camouflaging the very existence of the large corporation and the large organization? Where can you buy them?
- How do the professions assist senior corporate management in masking their activities from shareholders, staff, and the state – as well as the public.
- Is there anything to learn about camouflaging our *own* activities as researchers, and even as consumers, as we are observed by our senior management and that of interested corporations and the state apparatus?

It may well be best to conceptualise camouflage as being about a mode of confusing the observer *and* a mode of hiding from the observer. The former may be a version of the latter but for these purposes let us assume these two dimensions have different saliences.

Modes of Confusing

Here, for the analyst, organizational visibility is assumed but the nature of what is to be seen, and how it is interpreted, are issues for understanding the camouflaging process.

The first mode of confusing the casual observer we may wish to label is *Organizational Dazzle*. This is where there is an attempt to confuse the eye of the beholder by showiness, a 'look at the pretty lights' invitation, an attempt to hide the organization by it being bedecked with glittering superficialities. Dazzle hides the movement the organization wishes not to be seen, and allows the 'anaetheticization' of staff and clients to some issues through the countervailing medium of 'stunning' aesthetics which are both attention grabbing *and* allow the obscuring of details of activity that are best unseen by the customer. Disneyization is a classic example of this dazzling process as Alan Bryman (1999) and John Van Mannan (1991) showed us so well.

The second mode of confusing organizational realities is the *Masquerade*. Here the theme is the importance of the masked ball, which was *the* feature of the Baroque period. Apart from the hiding of identity behind the mask and costume, there is intense use of mirrors and hidden entrances. Backdoor arrangements, in other words, are fully developed so that clients are led through a 'set' without realizing just how constructed their passage is, and that it is for them specifically. An example here might be the company 'Enron' (Cruver 2003) and the fake dealing room the corporation developed to show to possible 'punters' what their organizational activities were and how busy the trading was – only it wasn't. It was a stage set, masking a hollow shell that performed a function of money-making that was entirely different from that advertised. Similarly, *The Times* reports on November 11, 2021 that 7000 companies were registered from only *five* London addresses to take advantage of the UK government's furlough scheme. These 'organizational forms' claimed £473 million between them, using 'formation agents' that set up companies and administer them on behalf of directors. These hidden entrances to new opportunities are currently being investigated by a special team within HMRC.

The third mode of confusion we may think of as resting in Nature and is that of the *Murmuration*. This is where starlings and similar birds gather in the evening before roosting, in which there is the hiding of the 'one' amongst the 'many' to maximize the possibility of escape from predators. The message here from the single entity is 'Don't pick on me, I'm just moving about normally, the same as everyone in my field'. One example of this form of confusion might be the Russell Group of British universities where membership of the 20-plus institutions allows each to hide behind the collective structure and process. Each Vice Chancellor in this group is able to say 'Don't pick on me' because they appear to take turns in 'leading' so-called 'reforms' to pensions and working conditions right across the sector. This allows these organizations to escape detailed observation of their own specific behaviours since they hide in the flocking behaviour of others. All agency, all choice, all responsibility is taken away by this cloaking device of trade association.

Fourth as a mode of confusion is a reliance upon *Name Changes*. Here, whilst the name changes, the organizational reality behind the shift in 'identity' remains the same. Thus, the corporate title 'P&O' replaced that of 'Townsend Thoresen' immediately after the sinking of the roll on-roll off ferry 'Herald of Free Enterprise' in Zeebrugge harbour in 1987 (Boyd 1990). Similarly, for those that seek to analyse the fortunes of the quasi-military firm 'Blackwater' which played such a large part in the US strategy immediately after the Iraq War, the company's many name changes thereafter, as it sought to cleanse its image of its alleged role in mass shootings of Iraqi citizens, is another example in point (Adubato 2011). I have already pointed to Facebook's name change to 'Meta' in late October 2021 at a time when the company was receiving a battering from legislative bodies around the world.

Fifth, we witness in the right-wing rhetoric concerning 'cancel culture' (Norris 2021) that those who claim their voice is being denied are often the most powerful in particular arenas. Those that state their interests are now being ridden over roughshod by groups and individuals who are particularly 'woke' are thereby given permission (by themselves) to act as if they are excluded and in need of being listened to intently and respectfully. This is a camouflage of confusion. The powerful claim they are silenced in order to be noisier than usual. They are supposedly cancelled from view but in complaining about their supposed exclusion they succeed in diverting attention from their underlying actions and mask what that really do. It is the trick of the conjuror.

We now turn to deeper undercover operations where the objective is more than just confusing the observer. It is actually about seeking to escape observation in any way whatsoever.

Modes of Hiding

The first of these attempts to escape any observation is *Mimicry*. Because the organization adopts the shape and colouration of pre-existing entities, it seeks to proffer the understatement that 'there is nothing different to see here'. This process of engaging in 'chameleon-ism' is clearly a form of camouflage. The objective is to strategically embrace isomorphism (from the Latin for 'identical shape') and appear to be content with a passive harmony with the environment, fitting into it unnoticeably and unremarkably. This is more than simply 'going with the flow' or being a 'late adopter' to market forces. What is meant here is a deliberate insertion of the corporation into an environment in which it will remain hidden because it has no clearly separable identity and its boundary is rendered invisible.

Second in the modes of hiding category is the science fiction injunction to put 'Shields Up'. This is the search for everyday stealth to be in operation. The trek for the invisibility cloak behind which to hide has been a well-recognized tool of organizations over the centuries. Keeping organizations secret has a long history (Domagal 2002; Anand et al. 2014). In a more recent mixed metaphor, operating 'stealthily' and 'below the radar' are both desirous of the discouragement of any observation by an outsider. Today, London Clubs offer 'gentlemen' (and rarely 'ladies') places where they can speak freely without fear of reports leaking into the outside world (Milne-Smith 2011). Honesty between such 'gentlemen' is made possible without the ear of the general public being exposed to one's thoughts. Similarly, the Freemasons (Parker 2016; Onnerfors 2017; Ferguson 2019) used to offer this sort of all-male protection from observation, and the British Treasury, even today, seeks to maintain this cloak of secrecy about its membership and its methods.

Next for our attention is the presence of many *Layers of Screening* as a mode of hiding. Taking the dramaturgical stage as our metaphor (Cornelisson 2004), many forms of management (re)presentations take place upon the many 'stages' upon which management works. Here we need to look out for veils, scene painting, and stage flies within which much is hidden, either upon the stage or behind it. The aim is to engender a willing suspension of disbelief within the observer because 'obstacled distance' between scene and viewer lends enchantment. The more we have to peer through layers to see the main stage, the less we observe on the periphery of the setting and that which lies in hiding. This method of hiding has been discussed earlier in the book.

Finally, there is out and out *Concealment* of the legal existence of organizations in trusts, multiple ownerships, and shareholdings of individual and organizational activity (Sikka 2013, 2015). This obfuscation is permitted by the legal system, the accounting system, and other related professions. In other words, put succinctly, much of the work of the Western professions is to hide, quite legitimately, the activities of the organizational world. So, unmasking the mode of hiding adopted by many organizations will require a close analysis of the world of the professions and professionals who inhabit it.

In conclusion, our theoretical object, 'organization', however defined, needs to be defended as a crucial component of the present system of financial-industrial capitalism, even one dominated by neo-liberalism's fixation upon the 'market' mechanism. The world is still organized by large organizations and departments of the State, often 'at a distance' and often through many forms of camouflage of the types we have just revealed.

Researching 'camouflage' is a possibility, even though it looks like an activity that is oxymoronic. More than this, however, is that this unmasking research is essential to modern Organization Theory.

So, as we saw earlier, there are at least six sets of reasons for the 'organization' to be deemed less salient than it was. But does this not miss the point? Simply because a skyscraper no longer proclaims its residents' presence through advertising hoardings and lights, we should not assume that the corporation has disappeared. This may be a carefully considered programme of camouflage to avoid responsibilities for the replacement of dangerous cladding, for example (Bulley and Brassett 2021). Organizations may be hiding themselves for particular reasons of seeking a deeply desired invisibility. Not least of which, of course, may well be to do with tax avoidance and even tax evasion (Chernykh and Mitakov 2017). Financialization (Epstein 2005; Lapavitsas 2011; Thompson 2013; Davis and Williams 2017) of many businesses, and even voluntary organizations, has meant that the 'company' of today is a financial shell in which little is actually 'made' and its administration is concerned with the movement of electronic money and very rarely real people and products (Jancsics 2017). The organization that is a financial shell still has a large number of accountants and lawyers within it, whom we should not forget. When a company is devoid of obvious contribution to the local economy, its presence may well be camouflaged in a plethora of legal holdings. This is not to say that it is beyond the reach of Organization Theory nor that it should be. It is merely to say that the invisibility of the organization should not fool us into ignoring it (Sikka 2015).

Similarly, the franchised firm may be a 'Moma and Papa' store but its franchising 'parent' is probably a very large entity (Alon et al. 2020). As Covid-19 has progressed in the USA, there has been a related non-stop evocation of the 'mom-and-pop landlord' – much like that of the 'small business owner' – in order to sanitize and romanticize the image of property ownership and enhance opposition to threatened legislation that would protect tenants from eviction (*Citations Needed* 2021). The 'parent' will require bureaucratic control of its franchisees through the need for widespread advertising schemes, costs and portion control of the products themselves, and the real desire to avoid reputational damage through, say, uncleanliness and severe customer illness. True, the nature of the day-to-day organization of activities may not be as well entrenched as 'direct control' was in the day of the large firm but it is still a form of 'responsible autonomy' (Friedmann 1990). Also, in using overseas production facilities, many garment companies have been able to subcontract their ethical responsibilities to processing zones across the world (Perry et al. 2015). In this way they can claim no knowledge of sweatshop labour and child exploitation, even though their quality control mechanisms (like the barbed wire fences around their processing zones) are razor sharp. In like manner, the organization of work under organizations such as Uber and Deliveroo is not devoid of bureaucracy. True, this type of organization is largely built into the algorithm behind the app but here is where so much administrative labour is to be found today. Organization Theory should hold its interest in algorithms, 'application' design, and use – and it does (Introna 2016; Introna and Nissenbaum 2000).

It is also highly noteworthy that Google, Apple, Amazon, and Facebook control much of the economic activity around the home and its needs. For anyone to claim that these are not huge bureaucratic organizations with clear organizational structures and systems and processes is to miss the centrality of these organizations to our lives both within and after Covid-19. The recognition and widespread critique of Amazon's role in France before 2020's 'Black Friday' shows that other cultures are well aware of the power of that particular company over a national culture. Of course, these companies are very visible and well discussed. But be aware, elements of their work are still masked, and many other organizations with less global reach are able to hide the vast majority of their activities behind many layers of camouflage.

Global–Local Contexts for Organizational Life

Organization Theory has embraced the search for an understanding of international capitalism, first associated with the rise of the Japanese economy in the 1980s and then China's climb, after a hiatus of 150 years, to its previous pre-eminence as the world's largest economy. Neither Japan nor China look like Anglo-American capitalism but neither, of course, do the Rhinish economies of Western Europe (Jessop 2012). Faced with a plethora of modes of organizing capitalism, a number of writers have sought to explain this diversity. First, we need to be clear that new institutional theory (already revealed as a dominant theoretical framework within Organization Theory at the present time) does not generally think about the sea of capitalism in which institutions swim. Nor does it tend to use the 'state' as a concept of high utility. For these reasons, the analysis of international capitalism has remained an area wherein institutional theory has not established itself with deep – or even shallow – roots (Davis and Marquis 2005). Second, regimes of capitalist accumulation require regimes of regulation (Aglietta 2000) and this is where organizations and organizing enter the picture more obviously. For Aglietta, post-war capitalism was based upon Fordist mass production, the Keynesian state, the family, and a centrally placed financial sector. But clearly, this is not enough in itself to bring organizations to the fore. Boyer's critique (2005) of Aglietta identified four types of regimes of accumulation; market-oriented capitalism, meso-corporatist capitalism, the French model of heavy involvement of the state in the economy, and social democratic capitalism. Boyer talks of the 'muddling through' that such regimes undertake in the face of world economic shocks. However, the centrality placed on large scale mass production of a Fordist kind was soon to be questioned (Amin 2011). For want of a better term, 'post-Fordism' came into heavy use and this notion was used to understand the organization of work, based upon flexible manufacturing in the industrial sectors, wherein intense accounting systems are in place in the search for profit. The firm, the organization, is the key unit of analysis here. Richard Whitley's (1987) interest in varieties of capitalism encouraged him to 'take the firm seriously as an economic actor'. He argued that, within the USA, the firm was seen as the dominant actor and as being emplaced in a sea of competition but held together by intense managerial coordination. The tightly knit firm of the USA has to be contrasted with the much looser relations found within Japanese (Gedajlovic et al. 2005) and South Korean business groups, as well as in Chinese family-based units. These cannot be represented in the classic pyramidal way because of all sorts of overlaps and partial participations. And in each national system there are a variety of ways in which overlapping networks change and alter arrangements over time.

What this suggests for Organization Theory is that there is a whole world to explore in terms of differences and similarities between regimes of accumulation and regulation, between firms and loose networks, between family-based units held together by enduring kinship, and entrepreneurial enterprises based solely around making money quickly and then selling off the entity when most valued by competitors. There is an entire globe to understand in terms of cultural and religious differences between systems at the international, national, and regional levels. Organization Theory appears to have a global and local pathway to further exploration laid out before it. All we need is some sensitivity as to how and in what ways these differences mask commonalities within the operation of financial capitalism.

However, the coming world of global organization may bring with it profound and regressive disadvantages for all who work within them. Organization Theory has pointed to worlds in which sadism, misogyny, cruelty, lack of trust, and enforced misery are to be found across the organized world (Seabright and Schminke 2002; Lencioni 2015). Whether one sees the child labourer in an Economic Processing Zone (Klein 2000) in the Philippines, manufacturing clothes to be sold on the high street, or on digital platforms of the West, or the ship-breakers on the beaches of India facing injury and death in their jobs every day, or the suicidal impulses felt by many Japanese white collar workers facing redundancy (Kitanka 2015; Mehri 2000), or the heart attacks suffered by US managers as they try to stay on top of their jobs and their staff, one is witnessing the costs of employment in firms by which the global economy is to be known (Lewchuk et al. 2006). Living lives governed by capitalist firms is one thing but the state is equally guilty in many societies for the same appalling treatment of its staff. Voluntary organizations would be better, one would hope, but here again Oxfam, for example, presided over sexual harassment and rape cases without pursuing the perpetrators or listening to the victims over many months (Carolei 2018; Cooper 2019). Organization Theory can be an upbeat approach to the topics in which it is interested. It can be taught with humour and enthusiasm (Cunlifffe and Luhman 2012). But behind this lies a dark world of pain and lack. Whilst we humans may have organized our lives for 100 centuries, based on a whole variety of ways of doing things, what we have in the twenty-first century is a narrow range of possibilities that we are told are possible – what I have called earlier, the 1 metre of wall. The real task for Organization Theory is to show how alternatives to bureaucratic centralized capitalism work and that they can work. But we will not get that historically based futurology from the Business Schools of the world. We need to organize ourselves differently, and quickly.

6 Organizing Differently

Blat, Peasants, and Indigenous Organizations

This chapter will consider the differing contexts for organizational life. As I suggested at the outset of this small book, we have to be choosy here and cannot possibly deal with all forms of alternatives to bureaucracy and formal organizing as recognized by social scientists. Our exploration of the 9-metre wall of possibilities can only be partial. I am going to deal with only three, albeit very important ones. These are organizing through *blat* and its relation to Western notions of 'corruption'; organizing through a peasant life style; and organizing through indigenous forms of relationship.

1. The clash of bureaucracy and blat in time/space

Part of conventional, or safe, Organization Theory is the accepted emphasis on shared Western values and their widespread promulgation overseas (Abreu-Pederzini and Suarez-Barraza 2020). The issue of corruption in large organizations, both in terms of their internal workings and their external relationships, has exercised those working in business ethics for many years (Nielsen 2003; Knouse et al. 2007). 'Corruption' suggests an infection of a corporate body that is so strong that it leads to inevitable dis-ease and decay. It is based to some extent upon a medieval sense of the body (Crossley 1995) and soul in which 'feeling bad' meant feeling ill. A predominant view is taken today that the world previously has been based upon bribery and corruption, but post-war internationalism heralds a new age of 'cleaning up' global interactions:

> Since the mid-1990s, the issue of corruption has gained a prominent place on the global agenda. International organizations, including the Organization for Economic Cooperation and Development (OECD) and the UN, have adopted conventions requiring that their members enact laws prohibiting bribery and extortion. International financial agencies, notably the World Bank, have announced programs aimed

DOI: 10.4324/9781003150503-6

at ensuring fair and open contracting for their projects and stopping misappropriation by government officials. Most nations have enacted some type of anticorruption law. International business groups have promulgated model codes of behavior, and multinational corporations (MNCs) now claim to be implementing antibribery programs.

(Worldwide Governance Indicators in
Kaufmann et al. 2010)

Corruption is placed here, within this quote, in relation to a seamless web of international trade organisations, MNCs, and nation states. These are linked by a commitment to rational bureaucratic modes of organizing through a shared global 'agenda'. A fabric of global, intermeshing networks exists in which the full might of the law, model codes of behaviour, and systematic programmes are deployed against corruption. We must note at this point that the great debate over the meaning and force of the 'rule of law' has also occurred within the same institutions since the early 1990s. The issues of the rule of law and anti-corruption are 'twinned' (Transparency International 2021).

Second, corruption and an absence of the rule of law are issues that are often associated with the rise of the BRIC economies in the early twenty-first century, placed by worried Western commentators (Gouvea et al. 2013; Windsor 2016) as existing outside of a Western (economic) hegemony. Third, corruption is also associated with 'failing states' and the 'war on terrorism', and with the supposed clash of cultures with Islamic versions of the 'law'. The problem here appears to be that some states are just too obviously lying outside of a Western political hegemony. Also noteworthy is a belief that 'corruption' is endemic within Latin America, Asia, and 'the Middle East'. Within these hegemonic views of economy and polity there is a tying-in of the rule of law with the 'ideal' bureaucratic mode of administration, a term which incidentally Weber never meant to imply such a hypothetical notion was the 'best' (Gerth and Mills 1957/2014). There is a clear assumption that 'rational-legal bureaucracy' (Townley 2008) is the way in which all international organizations should interact. It offers, allegedly, value freedom and no privileging of the lifestyles of the bureaucrats who work tirelessly, without fear or favour. At the same time, the assumption is made that not only do MNCs, nation states, and international trade organizations adopt fully bureaucratic systems; they also obey the rule of law.

The rule of law is seen in this discourse (Gouvea et al. 2013) as both a discursive product and a resource upon which groups may wish to draw. If I may say so, it is a 'plot' in both senses of the word. That is to say, the notion of 'the rule of law' is both a narrative drive *and* an orchestrated movement of political opportunism. Under the first sense, it is a measure of good governance and the quality of life; it is

> the extent to which agents have confidence and abide by the rules of society, and in particular the quality of contract enforcement, the police and the courts, as well as the likelihood of crime or violence.
>
> (Worldwide Governance Indicators; Kaufmann et al. 2010)

The plot in the first sense of the term then, is one of being a narrative drive, full of 'flows' inexorably towards the rule of law. For a while, China, Russia, Vietnam and so on were seen as increasingly embracing the rule of law in response to the excesses of the kleptocracies of the last 20 years. The future was bright. The future was less corrupt. The future looked more ethical.

What though of the *second* meaning of plot? Here one imagines advocacy of 'the rule of law' as an orchestrated movement representing political opportunism at the level of professional and business groupings. Look, for example, at the UN which defines 'the rule of law' as:

> a principle of governance in which all persons, institutions and entities, public and private, including the State itself, are accountable to laws that are publicly promulgated, equally enforced and independently adjudicated, and which are consistent with international human rights norms and standards. It requires, as well, measures to ensure adherence to the principles of supremacy of law, equality before the law, accountability to the law, fairness in the application of the law, separation of powers, participation in decision-making, legal certainty, avoidance of arbitrariness and procedural and legal transparency.

Inter alia, then, the cynic basing their view from within a critically based Organization Theory, might conclude that adherence to this UN principle seems to require a huge salariat dominated by lawyers. Compare this definition of the rule of law to that of Formal Bureaucracy which is also a principle of governance. There is adherence to the rule of law; behaviour is fair and principled and people act without fear or prejudice; authority derives from the office and not the person; there is specialization of function carried out by salaried administrative staff; the key emphasis is upon the keeping of written records. All of these elements require, to a greater of lesser extent, the involvement of and adjudication by professional lawyers.

Qui Bono is the question we might ask at this stage. Let us consider the 'World Justice Project' (Agrast et al. 2013). Formerly part of the American Bar Association, this group was set up in 2009 and became a free-standing non-profit organization. Its espoused aim is to promote adherence to the 'rule of law' throughout world and its actions and pronouncements are based on a definition of the 'rule of law' based on 16 factors with 68 sub factors. Essentially, laws are to be clear, publicized and stable, and access to law is provided by 'competent, independent and ethical adjudicators, attorneys and judicial officers who are of sufficient number, have adequate resources and reflect the makeup of the communities they serve'. Qui Bono indeed. The framework could be seen, maybe unfairly, as ensuring professional profit and as seeking professional promulgation.

The recent Western focus upon corruption and the attendant advocacy of the rule of law has as its targets, perhaps, those growing economies of the world which sit outside the western bloc, and act according to differing socio-economic principles. But such a focus also acts as a political wedge for the professional advancement of lawyers. This, it should be recognized, is no new phenomenon.

Writing and the Rule of Law

In the Peasant's Revolt of 1381, primarily in the south of England, it is apparent that the first thing the activists sought to achieve as they entered the bastions of the crown and of the aristocracy was the burning of all records. As McLynn (2012, p. 14) puts it, 'The hostility to lawyers, government officials and their archives and records was noteworthy'. This preceded looting of valuables in almost all cases. In Cambridge, the citizens joined in with the peasantry 'in gutting the university library and sacking Corpus Christi College', for the University was regarded as a 'blood sucking leech which practised academic freedom while colluding in local constraints upon urban and rural freedoms' (McLynn 2012, p. 45). Lawyers and those in control of writing were seen as opportunistically venal, for in maintaining the records, they had opportunities to rig the system firmly in their favour.

Four hundred years later, in France, the USA, Germany, England, and Scotland, for example, the Enlightenment was associated with the rise of 'the civilised man' (sic) and the dissolution of the old inequalities (Adorno and Horkheimer 1997). The key group within the Enlightenment might well be argued to be lawyers and those familiar with the law. With clients requiring skills in the acquisition and defence of property, the growth in the number and type of lawyers was fuelled by a market to represent the burgeoning bourgeoisie much more than the tiny number of aristocrats. Whilst the aristocracy in France was probably 1% of the population at the time of the Revolution, in Britain it was only 0.001%. And if the lawyers were to feel more at home with the company of the bourgeoisie than the aristocracy, they were also widely critical of religious clerics whose monopoly of Latin, the language of law, had prevented very little access to power from outside the clergy. Thus, the anti-clerical movement in the Enlightenment was often led by lawyers. Moreover, Parliamentary Government via a Commons is encouraged by the lawyers to circumvent the influence of the landed aristocracy, heavily ennobled as Lords.

Therefore, we have the following description of the legal establishment of the UK, originally stated in 1969 by John Griffith, whose concern for the functions of the rule of law should not pass us by:

> The rule of law is a fantasy invented by the Liberals of the old school and patented by the Tories to throw a protective sanctity around certain legal and political institutions and principles which they wish to preserve at any cost.

(Griffith 1977)

Here then, in this opportunistic sense of 'plot' we have a Western quadrilateral of huge significance which forms the 'conventional' organizational world for many people. There is, at each corner, the Enlightenment, bureaucracy, the rule of law, and lawyers. From this quadrilateral comes *one* understanding of corruption, widespread in the West. Its locus of power is the law courts of Washington, DC. It is important to note that Adorno and Horkheimer, in *The Concept of Enlightenment* (1972, p. 37 italics added) recognize this emphasis within the centuries since the Enlightenment:

> Domination, ever since men settled down, and later in the commodity society, has become objectified as law and organisation and *must therefore restrict itself*

What lies, we might ask, outside this restriction of law and organization? Are there those places and times where one or more of the 'restrictive' quadrilateral of forces is missing? Where the Enlightenment did not prevail (e.g. Southern Europe)? Where rational bureaucracy did not displace religious, value-based systems and where the rule of law is not 'yet' accepted (Saudi Arabia and the Gulf)? Where lawyers are not in a high-status profession (everywhere around the globe where the *West Wing* was not a huge success)? At this point let us consider places where the quadrilateral around legal bureaucracy is absent. I wish here to turn to the old Soviet Union and the 'new' Russia.

My argument will be that within the 'blat' model of governance, corruption as a concept tends to lose its valency. To develop this argument, we will consider Alena Ledeneva's three books on the same topic (1998, 2000, 2003) with particular focus upon the first, namely *Russia's Economy of Favours* (1998). Her focus is not upon the Washington law courts but the apartment blocks of Moscow. Herein, different linguistic codes are used within blat to describe certain types of relationship, but they originate within the speaker's particular macro- and micro-societal arrangements. Definitions-in-use in these tower blocks have a moral and highly judgemental nature. So, one declension of blat goes as follows; I support my friends, you buy favours, he is corrupt; we are one big family, you only look after your own, they are avaricious predators. According to Ledeneva (1998), blat enters Russian language usage via the city of Odessa as a term drawn from Yiddish and Polish. Variously it means 'illicitly, by protection, by patronage' or 'by acquaintance' or 'someone who provides an umbrella' or 'close, familiar', or 'a speaker of shared jargon'. It was definitely 'about obtaining more than it was about buying'.

Blat in practice was essentially a gift relationship *not* one based upon contract. It was centred upon who you know *not* what you know. Its underlying logic was of the family *not* of individual benefit. Its logical binaries focused upon ins *not* outs, brothers *not* strangers, family *not* predators. It emphasizes future favours and inner duties *not* immediate benefits; long-term bonds *not* short-term pleasures; deference, prestige, and authority *not* the amassing of wealth. Blat consists of both a vertical and a horizontal dimension to those who understand it. On the *vertical* plane there are those of differing status. These are 'useful' people with whom interactions are intermittent but instrumental. However, on the *horizontal* plane are those of similar status. These are 'people of the circle', they have similar values, needs, and expectations and crucially, the circle is closed to those without introduction. A non-Russian here might say well, blat is indistinguishable from everyday social interaction almost everywhere. But they would not go on, would they (?), to say that one's life was entirely organized this way – as it is under blat.

A professional dealer in blat was called a *tolkach*. 'It was their job to bypass bureaucratic snarl ups. A *tolkach* earned his keep by having good contacts; by being skilled in manipulating people, procedures and paperwork' (Nove 1977). For Ledeneva (1998, p. 37) 'they provide access to public resources through personal channels'. The *tolkach* therefore offers 'the favour of access' and they provide introductions. Thus, the relationship may not be dyadic but may involve a wide circle of mutual reciprocity. Ledeneva claims (1998, p. 36) that 'Soviet blat was similar to *guanxi* in China (Yang 1994) or *zalatwic sprawny* in Poland (Wedel 1986) but has no direct analogy in the West'. I beg to differ.

Remembering the need to pay attention to 'the speaker's particular macro- and micro-societal arrangements' when dealing with these issues, I wish to address a case which hopefully illuminates the role of blat at the level of the state, the organization, and the personal. I present to you Mr Mather. Mr Mather was the local *tolkach* in a North East coal mining village in 1959 when our story takes place. He was Labour County Councillor for Northumberland and a highly respected local teacher – 'a man of acquaint-ances and connections'. What follows is a personal story, yet it is a story of the bureaucratic state and a story of the organization of the community that must have been common in the UK at that time. I think it is a story which demonstrates the existence of blat in twentieth-century Britain.

As a person who had to sit the so-called 11+ examination, one was asked to nominate which grammar school one would like to attend if successful. I nominated Bedlington Grammar School which my sister had attended. When the result arrived with the allocation of a school, my friend and I had been put on the list of Morpeth Grammar School, not Bedlington. I was somewhat unhappy. My father said my friend and I should visit Mr Mather to see whether he could change the allocation. He was a County Councillor and should have some influence on matters educational. We turned up as two 11-year-old boys without appointment to Mr Mather's house on a Saturday morning. He had taught us the year before and so knew us both. He welcomed us into his house and listened carefully. At the end of our plea for movement, he said he would try and rectify the situation. We should expect a letter from Northumberland Education Authority in a few weeks. Today, in 2021, this informal request would be seen as totally illegitimate. Millions of people do not know County Council representatives and have to accept, without question, what they are allocated in terms of schools at the age of 11. A letter duly arrived and told us that we should go to Morpeth for a year in the first instance, and if we were unhappy at end of that year, a transfer to Bedlington would be forthcoming. Needless to say, after a happy year in a good school, neither of us wished to transfer.

If we see Mr Mather as the *tolkach* in this 1950s environment, which my father certainly did, we should ask the question: what was in it for our teacher? Did it inspire deference, a sense of his patronage, a vote for him in the next local election; did it raise his status, his prestige by showing his power; did it seek some form of reciprocity in the future? One thing is clear. By the standards of the day in this coal mining village this was not seen as a form of corruption. It was normal behaviour. And this is the problem with lawyerly definitions of 'corruption' that ignore communal and collective understandings based upon tradition.

In the very next parliamentary constituency, however, the law did find examples of corruption in the contracting out of large building projects. In Eddie Milne's autobiographical *No Shining Armour: the story of one man's fight against corruption in public life* (1976) there are clear examples of what were regarded at the time by the outgoing Labour MP as corruption.

This is typical when there is basically one-party government with ultra-safe seats for MPs and councillors. In these circumstances, whatever party is in national and local government, the rule of silence within the community tends to operate. In Mafia terms, this is known as the rule of 'omerta' (New Statesman 1973). The penalties for 'whistle-blowing' are very severe as Milne's story would show. He played (or was allowed to play) no further part in national or local political life.

Now as I have been at pains to point out, these examples are from the second half of the twentieth century, so does this mean that blat has disappeared from the UK landscape? Probably not. In the UK theatre industry, for example, there is a huge over-provision of labour and personal connections are deemed totally necessary to get one's first 'big break'. Family connections around internships at large corporations is endemic in the UK economy. The UK was rated only 11th in the world for anti-corruption in 2020 by Transparency International (2021). The USA was placed 25th. Members of the Tory Party in 2020–2021 have come close to saying that blat was essential in responding to the pandemic in order to circumvent the constraints of the system. Thus, blat is by no means only to be found in the left-wing regimes of the previous soviet or socialist societies. It is central to many 'western' 'capitalist' economies. Yet, is it theorized within Organization Studies? It is not.

There are four conceptual possibilities for the relationship between blat and bureaucracy that could be represented here spatially. They may be highly discrete, separate, and different spheres, or they may be seen as two overlapping worlds of self-creation. Imagine, if you will, Venn diagrams of a very simple kind. First, we might imagine that blat lies fully within the boundaries of bureaucracy as pockets of 'corruption' that need eradicating. Blat is the 'underworld' to bureaucracy's dominant reality. It is separate but subordinate and is policed heavily. In the contemporary USA this is the conventional view of 'illegal immigration' and many other forms of 'problematic' social life. Blat may also be seen as existing as an enclave in a sea of bureaucracy but as welcomed by significant numbers of people because of the protection it offers them. For example, Colin Williams' work on Sheffield (2007) demonstrates this possibility. Blat and bureaucracy are presented as inhabiting separate spheres. Citizens live within one **or** the other in some form of informal apartheid but recognize that they would be disadvantaged by inhabiting, or even visiting, the other.

Second, and more unexpectedly, it may be that bureaucracy lies fully within blat's boundaries and is an internal force for progress via the spread of the rule of law from within a world of corruption and pre-bureaucratic forms of administration, as described in so much detail by Max Weber (Gerth and Mills 1957/2014). If bureaucracy exists in a sea of blat at the international level, then we are speaking, within conventional Organization Theory, of Western Exceptionalism – and of course its fellow traveller – Western superiority. Blat is in the past, and the 'End of History' (Fukuyama 2006) ensures the future is based entirely upon the triumph of the rule of law.

However, from outside conventional approaches, it may well be true that bureaucracy exists in a sea of blat, *guanxi*, etc, *but* will never succeed in overthrowing traditional methods of organizing. If this spatial model is the best descriptor of the organized world, bureaucracy and the rule of law are both *minority* orientations. Billions of people on the planet prefer the protection offered by a locally based blat, rather than that offered by a national level formal and legal bureaucracy. Blat provides services, access, and resources that bureaucrats fail to deliver – indeed often cannot deliver. Within this unconventional, even 'edgy' approach, 'corruption' is, in part, an imperialist discursive notion promulgating the spread of the rule of law to advantage Western economic and political power, particularly as operationalized by some lawyers and parliamentarians. It faces a world of billions of people in which in order to get by, varieties of blat predominate their lives. The rule of law is an obstacle to them, and their families, thriving. Might it be then that bureaucracy, the rule of law, and international lawyers are all dying concepts of the twenty-first century? The discourse of the once powerful Enlightenment, which provided the bedrock upon which Organization Theory arose, is perhaps, ebbing away in a blat from the past.

To be more balanced, however, about the role of the legal profession in contemporary organizational life, we should note that the Tory Government in Britain has recently cut funding for the carrying out of reasonable and just legal proceedings with the abandonment of legal aid and the reduction of numbers at high levels in the judiciary. Simultaneously, as argued earlier, legal-rational means of making decisions and the keeping of records have been abandoned in the pandemic. Because blat exists, and there are problems with the way the professions engage with the rule of law, does *not* mean that this author is necessarily advocating an end to legal-rational forms of domination (Townley 1997,2002). I merely seek a wider and deeper understanding of the organizational consequences of the ways in which, and by which, we live.

2. A peasant mode of existence

I have spent a number of years arguing that the peasantry is 'the ghost at the table' within business and management studies (Burrell 1997, 2020). My concern for this social grouping is partly personal, for I come from a long line of 'ag-labs' (shorthand in genealogy for 'agricultural labourers') myself, and partly because a consideration of their lives widens out the history, geography, politics, and sociology of the present. The peasantry should be central to the social sciences but typically they are not. Attitudes to these peoples are often academically dismissive.

Defining the 'peasantry' across time and space is extremely difficult. It may be a European concept that travels very badly in Asia, never mind Africa. Its use is often associated with a colonial urge to render the colonized understandable within terms the colonizer understands. For that reason, we must tread extremely carefully. My working definition of the peasantry is 'rural cultivators who produce for subsistence and the market, using family labour and little capital, and for whom non-market considerations are crucial'. I begin by abandoning a theoretical position found within a standardized universal model of both the political 'left' and the 'right' that the peasantry will disappear because of an agrarian revolution, schisms in the structure of agriculture, and their incorporation into a proletarian class. As a consequence, travelling across the political spectrum reveals a shared assumption that whilst they exist, they are a drag on economic and political development. But their existence will be part of the End of History for it is clear (allegedly) that their days are numbered. Yet this claim has been harboured for centuries!

For example, Eric Hobsbawm (1994, p. 289) wrote that 'the most dramatic and far-reaching social change of the second half of this (last) century, and the one which cuts us off for ever from the world of the past, is the death of the peasantry'. Therefore, were we to follow Hobsbawm within Organization Theory, we need not worry about our neglect of the peasantry for they are surely vestigial, mortally wounded, due for extinction, a compromized evolutionary category (Lowy and Lowy 2000)?

Stereotypically, peasant life is seen as primitive and irrational, producing a class of barbarians supposedly tortured by everyday miseries. Indeed, instead of forming a class, peasants are portrayed as individualistic and to be seen as an agglomeration and nothing more. The peasant survives only by superhuman labour and sub-human life. They live in a 'semi-feudal' family subsistence type of economy where animal husbandry from half subterranean hovels had and has to be replaced by new industry in large sunlit factories. Karl Marx thus lumped them in with the 'petty bourgeoisie' as an unstable reactionary class 'halfway out of society'. They were not in the vanguard of revolutionary progress, indeed for some they were not even a rear-guard. For others, they were not even camp followers. To Pro-Industrializers of all parties of 'modernity', they were and are the atavistic *enemy* – with a lifestyle that must be eliminated. Max Weber in his writings, for example, advocated 'de-peasantization' because they were a deep pool of non-rationality. Moreover, the peasantry

Organizing Differently 57

is 'most lacking in culture' (Gerth and Mills 1957/2014, p. 368). They engage in 'primal, naturalist and unsublimated sexuality' (p. 349). They 'have been inclined towards magic' since 'they are bound to nature and depend upon elemental forces' (p. 283). They have not been trained 'to produce in order to gain profit' (p. 365). In other words, rationality has escaped the European peasantry in the face of their 2000 years of tradition and of conservatism.

There was, and is, an advocacy of de-peasantization from the (Neo) Liberals too, in order for the process of proletarianization of agricultural labour, collectivization of the land into massive, mega-productive units and large-scale mechanization, all within a 'propertyless' concept of the farm labourer, to go on unchecked. Untying their connection with particular plots of land 'freed' them up to move where they were needed in both the annual agricultural round and across the national landscape.

On yet another hand, there was also an advocacy of de-peasantization from Engels. He states (Engels 1976, p. 16)

Farm labourers can be rescued from their hideous misery only when, primarily, their chief object of labour, the land itself, is withdrawn from the private ownership of the big peasants and the still bigger feudal lords, transformed into public property and cultivated by co-operative associations of agricultural workers on their own account.

The agricultural proletariat – farm labourers – which is split and scattered, is the class nearest to the industrial proletariat. It is, politically, a 'sack of potatoes'. The peasantry is a heavy drag, then, to both Liberals and Socialists and all points in between.

However, is this widespread neglect of the peasantry within the social sciences of the twenty-first century warranted? An Associate Dean of Lancaster University School of Management said in answer to my espoused research question of why had Organization Theory ignored the peasantry, 'It's obvious isn't it. Because they have no money'. In so doing, he was echoing Marx (in Katz 1992) who characterized the French peasantry at the time of the mid-1850s thus, 'Their field of production, the small-holding, admits of no division of labour in its cultivation, no application of science and, therefore, no diversity of development, no variety of talent, no wealth of social relationships'. They were powerless and lived outside capitalism's future. Van der Ploeg (2010, p. 20) maintains that the first editorial of the *Journal of Peasant Studies* referred to peasants as 'the most underprivileged', although it also referred to their 'long [...] history of struggle against such conditions' (Byres et al. 1973). In the same issue, Hobsbawm (1973, p. 7) discussed the 'general subalternity of the peasant world' claiming that 'peasantness' was defined by 'subalternity, poverty, exploitation and oppression'.

Jim Handy (2009) in the *Journal of Peasant Studies* wrote a piece suggestively subtitled 'A long history of blaming peasants'. In it, he specifically cites *The Economist* of 1841 as the source of much of the vilification of the peasantry by business, and of constructing anti-peasant rhetoric. A Belfast reporter described, without pity, filthy wretches living like swine – indeed living *with* swine – in a one-roomed hovel in rural Ireland. Yet the English prosperity of the 1840s, described and valorized by *The Economist* was built upon the extreme immiseration and impoverishment of the Irish farm labourer. Therefore, it is not that clear that the 'landed aristocracy' welcomed the breakdown of the old semi-feudal ways to the same extent as industrialists did in the nineteenth century. The former were very happy with social arrangements as they were. The latter required free labour to move to and between their factories. Yet, here we are today, despite the best efforts of the agents of industrial capitalism, with three billion peasants still working upon the land.

My argument is that the 'peasantry' *appear* to be absent in Business and Management Studies in general, and in Organization Theory in particular, because the focus for 150 years has been upon the industrial and commercial sectors of an industrial or post-industrial economy. Their rural lifestyle, location in the primary sector of what might be thought to be close to a feudal economy, commitment to traditional patterns of belief and authority especially witchcraft, particular conceptions of time and space, illiteracy, oral histories, a focus often upon bare survival, and in places a commitment to blat and *guanxi* forms of relationships all mark them as different from industrial workers. They have been camouflaged from the wider 'advanced' economy, not so much by their own efforts (although these might not be insignificant), but by being rendered invisible to the powerful. Nowhere is this clearer than in the use of derogatory terms for 'the peasant' across many nations which reflects their low status in urban, metropolitan, science-based cultures. 'Villains' all. And no one wants to be associated with 'clod-hoppers' for they are *soiled*. The peasantry are seen as matter out of place – 'dirt' – to be shunned by even the academy, since the assumption is widespread that our status as academics comes from that which we research. Thus, Organization Theory is seen by those in Strategic Management as inferior, since they deal, allegedly, with senior management. Organization Theorists only reach middle management levels in seeking social advancement through their subject matter. Researching the peasantry is *infra dig*.

Yet, the peasantry remain key parts of the world's social system amounting to billions of human beings in the twenty-first century. However,

'Almost half of the people in the world are peasants' (*Via Campesina*, The Peasant Way 2008; Torrez 2011). The suggestively named Van der Ploeg (2010, p. 29) maintains that

> In 1970 the world's agricultural population stood at 2.0 billion, while by 2010 it will have grown to 2.6 billion. Phrasing it differently, agriculture directly supports the livelihoods of more than three billion people.
> (data derived from Borras 2009, p. 15)

He goes on to state that the peasantry is not a vestige of the old; it is a social grouping that has undergone not one history but many, so its linkages with the present are not unilinear but complex. Thus, for Van de Ploeg, the peasantry is in 'process' and moreover, in the current Climate Crisis discussions, land is back on the agenda as it is 'self-provisioning'. Similarly, Akram-Lodhi and Kay (2010, p. 280) maintain (albeit within a torrent of unfamiliar terms) that

> On the contrary "...the renewed relevance of the agrarian question is witnessed in postsocialist repeasantisation through decollectivisation; semi-proletarianisation and fragmentation without full proletarianisation as livelihood strategies reconfigure; the remarkable stability in the absolute number of peasant farmers over the last 40 years; the continued importance of smallholder food production to rural livelihoods in much of the South; the deepening of the market imperative and the law of value across the world capitalist economy under neoliberal globalisation, with implications for capitalist agriculture and petty commodity producing peasant farming; the expanded commodification of natural resources, including land, labour-power and genetic resources.

Yet, attempts have been made, successfully, to de-peasantize societies. These are often through *coercion*. First, there are enclosures and forcible clearances of labourers from the land. The British legal establishment in the eighteenth century were quite adept at entering Parliament as MPs and sometimes, once in office, pointed to the absence of legal documents held by the peasantry to legitimate their land holdings. Without a deed, enclosure of peasant land became much easier. There was also the process of mechanizing the land with steam and petrol driven machines. Once off the land, peasant-based senses of temporality were in need of immediate replacement. Their sense of 'Kiros' (subjective time) was to be replaced with 'chronos' (objective, clock-based time). In case they wished to return to the land on experiencing industrial work for the first time, their places of employment became prison factories. These were augmented with police regimes, in the factories of Ford and in Japanese textile mills most notably, where labour turnover was translated as 'escape'. The newly industrializing peasantry were held rigid in work 'stations' and forced emplacement without possible egress – as recent factory fires in Bangladesh still demonstrate.

Taylorism is a defining moment of de-peasantization, for his system provided a semi-successful set of procedures for taking a peasant 'in hand' and making a proletarian through specific work practices. Precisely the same techniques are now being employed, for example, in Vietnam, the Philippines, Thailand as well as in the PRC and India. Within export processing zones (Milberg and Amenguel 2008), the nation state is seen as not in effective control nor is legal action within the boundary of the huge compounds possible, so the newly incoming factory worker finds themselves 'outside' of all societal norms (Cairns 2007) and legal protections. In North America, NAFTA (Robert 2016) was estimated in its first 10 years to have forced 6 million poor farmers off the land in Mexico. In return, 6 million tons of GM corn is exported south annually. It is Terminator seed which goes sterile after one season. It is estimated that 1.3 million small farmers plus their families have moved to the USA with the help of 'travel agencies' which often dump them in Arizona without shelter, jobs, or documentation. So, without putting too fine a point on it, de-peasantization goes ahead to fill the vacant jobs of gardeners and nannies to the rich across the Rio Grande (Payan 2016).

Organization Theory needs to consider these forces before the peasant enters the labour market of a bureaucratically organized society. How are the peasantry (pre-)organized? In what ways does their communitarianism express itself? Can we ever understand the labour of others with our own categories of 'employment' and 'career' (Savickas 2010)?

To take but one example, writing from her position in India as leader of SEWA, (the Self-Employed Women's Association) Bhatt (2004, p. 17) tells us the following example is a common one and as such it must challenge our conventional understandings of organized labour:

> A small farmer works on her own farm. In tough times, she also works on other farms as a labourer. When the agriculture season is over, she goes to the forest to collect gum and other forest produce. Year round, she produces embroidered items either at a piece rate for a contractor or for sale to a trader who comes to her village to buy goods. Now how should her work be categorized? Does she belong to the agricultural sector, the factory sector or the home-based sector? Should she be categorized as farmer or a farm worker. Is she self employed or is she a piece rate worker?

Bhatt argues that because this person's situation cannot be easily defined, she has no work status, is denied access to training or financial services, and has no 'identity' within the economy. The peasant, even if they wanted to, cannot move easily to the status of employee if they have to travel through this 'intermediate' set of stages of being **in** the economy but not accepted as being *of* the economy. This then, to Western eyes, is some 'intermediate' position of pluriactivity (Van Der Ploeg 2008, pp. 32–33), in which work on the land, in the home, and outside the home on other premises is possible. Pluriactivity is a partial solution to survival for the family is the basic social unit and its objective is survival not monetary returns.

Bhatt and Jhabvala (2012, pp. 1–2) point out that

> Indian labour laws view work as a relationship between an employer and an employee. In this model of industrial relations, the worker is considered "an industrial man", a worker with one formal contract, regular working hours and a living wage. In the Indian context this leaves out 90% of our workers, who have no fixed employer-employee relationship, no fixed place of work, and who do many kinds of work, often in the same day, or season to season.

It is understandable, then, why Organization Theory should neglect the peasantry, given two primary features: first, their position within the intellectual history of the West is seen as one of impending demise and imminent transfer into the status of 'employee' or proletarian; and second, the mysterious ways in which the peasantry appear to live outside bureaucratic, industrial, capitalistic, and legal-rational modes of organization. This, however, is by no means a nineteenth-, twentieth-, or twenty-first-century issue.

As we have seen already within revolts of the peasantry, the written word upon stored documents, is their first target for destruction. The peasantry have lived lives independent of many dominant regimes of regulation for millennia, and apparently in most circumstances (though not all) wish to maintain this distance. The State Museums of Vienna and Berlin hold examples of home-made weapons manufactured by the land labourers in the Peasant Revolts of the fourteenth and sixteenth centuries. They are fearsome pieces of militaria and should remind us (notwithstanding a reputation for quietism) that the peasantry are capable of collective action in pursuit of their own goals. And the fact that the peasantry remain key parts of the world's social system amounting to billions of human beings in the twenty-first century should prick our interest in their organizing as independent of the (or should one say 'a') world of organization that many of us consider to be significant (or even essential).

3. Indigenous forms of organizing

Another form of organizing that lies outside the understanding and gaze of conventional Organization Theory is 'Indigenous Organization Studies' (Love 2018). Here, a key source is Tyron Rakeiora Love's book of that title, its subtitle being 'Exploring Management, Business and Community' and in the last word is its key difference from the Western norm. Love argues that a new field needs to be developed within Organization Theory whereby indigenous peoples would be placed at the centre of one's research, and to encourage it to consider how workplaces might be changed when indigenous organizing principles were adopted. 'Research' from within conventional Organization Theory has had a bad reputation for many years (Smith 2021), for indigenous people become treated as a resource for the publications, and ultimately the career, of non-indigenous research academics. Such academic work is greeted with disdain and resistance by those upon whom it is practised. Therefore, someone who is outside of these communities in New Zealand, the Pacific Islands, Canada, the USA, Australia, and Sub-Artic Europe, as well as indigenous communities within Africa and Asia, and the indigenous peoples of Chile, Mexico, and Ecquador, must tread with extreme caution. Just as we cannot claim to fully understand peasant lifestyles (or even, partially), then looking at indigenous peoples around the world carries many difficult obstacles for the outsider.

Love (2018, pp. 8–9) argues that Indigenous Organization Studies differs from Organization Studies by virtue, firstly, of its reluctance to accept the natural/social science divide that is so familiar to most readers. Indigenous knowledges are about an enduring connection between peoples and the land and a heavy dependence upon ancestral knowledge. The land/place connection is paramount in most indigenous cultures. There is believed to be an ancient covenant with plants, animals, and the earth, each imbued with a spirit in which energy waves, constant motion, and flux and renewal are key dimensions. Compared to this world view, Organization Theory in its conventional sense appears not to bother itself with local knowledge and native ways of both living in the world to conserve resources, and in expressing intimate and communal problems as central.

Love maintains that the way forward for Indigenous Organization Studies is to embrace the discourses and narratives within indigenous communities. Discourse approaches are held to be important because they draw attention to the constructive effects of language and the dominance of particular frames of reference, even when employed way outside of their usual domain. Narratives and stories are 'essential to indigenous ways of knowing' in 'active, contextualised and living ways' (Love 2018, p. 19). Love seeks to build bridges with Organization Studies in its more conventional rendering by addressing the work of David Boje (2016), Yiannis Gabriel (1999, 2015), and Barbara Czarniawska (2008). This bridge building works less well in my view.

For example, 'Reflexive Hermeneutics' is a set of ideas that has been taken up in the twenty-first century within the study of 'organizing' by Cunliffe, Kuhman, and Boje (2004). They use Ricoeur's *Time and Narrative* and attempt to fuse it with some ideas from Sartre's *Being and Nothingness* in order to bring forth a theory of narrative temporality (NT). The aim of NT is to develop a particular branch of narrative organizational research in which organizational life is seen as a 'negotiated, synchronic and polyphonic' (Cunliffe et al. 2004, p. 262) where the hermeneutic task is to interpret one's own interpretations and to subject one's own authority as interpreter and author to auto-critique. Emphasis is on the 'moment to moment' reciprocity of speaking and listening to oneself and others. For 'stories are not just chronologies (a sequence of events) but situated, responsive performances' (ibid, p. 273) creating a multiplicity of pasts, presents, and futures. One method of achieving narrative temporality approaches to organizational life for these authors might be through 'social poetics' where this performance element, its use of intra-linguistic practices, and its bodily reflection are seen as the focus of attention. But, whilst Love appears to see and seek the 'long duree' in indigenous narratives, Cunliffe et al. (2004) wish to emphasise its short-lived nature; in other words, its temporality. I suspect these differing emphases would take Indigenous Organization Studies off in a direction that Love would find lacking in much utility (see, for example, Love 2018, p. 21).

It is clear that computer-based 'search engines' reflect back what we appear to be looking for and so constrain our questioning in dramatic ways (Simpson 2012). They give us what *they* think we want. Similarly, Boje (2019) points to the very shallow forms of interviewing that cannot be accepted as decent methodological practice when they really disadvantage indigenous cultures. What the interviewer wants to hear may not be what the interviewed think they want to say. Especially if it is in translation. There is a power asymmetry in methods just as there is a power asymmetry in theory. Love seems to bypass this inconvenience in utilizing the sources that are cited.

In a very challenging way, Love (2018, pp. 32–33) speaks of 'indigenous entrepreneurship'. Being fed a diet of entrepreneurship in the business school world of the UK has allowed me to be very snooty about this topic and to rail against the overblown claims for what it does, and what is has achieved. However, once one reads the material dealt with, and contributed to, by Love (for example, Nandu-Templeton et al. 2017;

Scheyvens et al. 2017) one's viewpoint is changed. And this is precisely the reason for those of us on the 'outside' to contemplate embracing Indigenous Organization Studies. It is an approach which re-orients one to a better understanding of that which we know not.

Thus, by way of example, Maori-centred entrepreneurship retains indigenous membership and identities, engages in reciprocity, maintains Maori control of people, place, and land, and of keeping a view of the spirituality of the life forces in the community at the forefront of the organization (Case and Gosling 2010). Fishing communities reflect entrepreneurship in their respect for differing time horizons to do with seasons and tides. The commonality of shared meaning over time is important here (perhaps *contra* the work of David Boje, Yiannis Gabriel, and Barbara Czarniawska). Love argues that the stranger is not a good researcher, for pre-understandings of these cultures is crucially important. So too, is the question of the research's usefulness. There is no question to writers within indigenous Organization Studies that research should be useful to the population and its values (Love 2018, p. 41). That is not always the case in conventional Organization Studies.

The really important issue here is the fact that Indigenous Organization Studies relates, in the vast majority of cases, to a colonized people. Decolonial and anti-colonial discourses (Singh 2017) have been interrelated to Indigenous Organization Studies because the politics and power relationships within academia on these issues is very intense. Theory has oppressed many peoples across the world (Turner 2004). The usual portrayal of Maoris, for example, from within a colonially-based narrative, is often that they are 'lazy', lack a regard for time, and are unreliable (Love 2018, p. 55). However, time is perceived differently within Maori culture for it is about discussion and building collective consensus. This sort of perspective places Indigenous Organization Studies on the edge of the conventional world of Organization Theory. It appears to represent a 'language of the vanquished' (Alvarado 2009, p. 304) that has now slipped into the past. Just as the peasantry (who may well be indigenous, of course) are supposed to have done.

In this chapter I have focussed upon three areas of difference between conventional Organization Theory and what I think needs to be researched in a development of the discipline. These areas of 'Indigenous Organization Studies'; a concern for the significance of the peasantry with business and management and social science more generally; and for understanding the issues of blat (and its cousins) as key to comprehending bureaucracy and the rule of law upon which it is based, are by no means comprehensive. Other issues should claim our attention, but space here is pressing. And there is one more chapter in which we can push out from our self-imposed constraints.

7   Beyond Conventional
Organization Theory

This, then, is where we move outward to edgy organization theory, the antithesis in some ways of safe, conventional Organization Theory (Grey and Willmott 2005; Casey 2002; Frost 1980). Herein, Granter and McCann (2015) have pointed to 'edgework' (Lyng 1990) and its dangers, often in a physical sense, from one's object of study. They say that 'The vividness of the data generated in such research settings is a potent draw for ethnographers looking to document extreme, emotionally-laden and generally unforgiving lifeworlds that lie outside a more "mainstream" habitus'. Attention is paid by Granter and McCann and their colleagues to unusual, strange, emotionally intense, dangerous, and deviant activities that have always been major features of social research. These actions involve risk and/or possible threat to life. Here, however, I concern myself with dangers merely to a career – but for the Organization Theorist, edgework is undoubtedly unusual, strange, and deviant.

What is meant by this term 'edgy' has yet to appear in the Oxford English Dictionary, even though it is to be found colloquially. The fact that it is, as yet, undefined by major dictionaries makes it somewhat attractive to me in this context. It is meant to represent something that is both on the 'edge' of the mainstream *and* is capable of sharply cutting that of which it is a peripheral part. It also refers, perhaps, to the possibility that a fall from an unstable position is more than possible because of being out on a limb, far from safety. Now, as I said earlier, this is a problematic boundary because it is a simple binary with all the problems that are attendant upon that. Placed on one side of the Rubicon has been a 'safe Organization Theory'. Across the river, across the border, on the other side, we might find 'edgy Organization Theory'. Many of my colleagues, who would be very unhappy with the notion that they were engaging in dialectics, would point out that several intermediate positions are possible within this particular binary. These alternatives are in the 'contact zone' between the binary points where we might expect to contact 'hybrids'. Anna Tsing's work on 'friction':

DOI: 10.4324/9781003150503-7

the 'awkward, unequal, unstable and creative qualities of interconnection across difference' – through which 'cultures are continually co-produced' (Tsing 2011, p. 4) might be seen as a way forward in understanding 'intermediate' positions. However, Yunkaporta (2019, p. 233) has pointed out that power relations are so skewed that 'there is not much opportunity for the brackish waters of hybridity to stew up something exciting'.

If this is correct, there is still the binary problem of whether to stay within Conventional Organization Theory, or whether to go beyond the pale. This transgression is the essence of the story of the crossing of the Rubicon by Julius Caesar in January 49 BC (Beneker 2011):

> He came upon his cohorts at the River Rubicon which was the boundary of his province, and stopped briefly. As he considered the magnitude of his undertaking, he turned to his companions and said "Even now, we can turn back, but once we have crossed this little bridge, everything will have to be settled by fighting".
>
> (Suetonius 31.2)

Settling by Fighting

Crossing the bridge out of conventional Organization Theory will bring about fractious dispute that will involve fighting. As Mike Reed and I argued recently (Reed and Burrell 2019)

> The constant search for disciplinary control is now re-emerging as a project to convert organization studies' academic community into a hegemon-controlled discipline via profound ideological and intellectual closure around the field's focus, agenda and form. We suggest that if they have their way in 'celebrating Organization Theory' (Lounsbury and Beckman 2015; Davis 2015), our current institutional thought leaders will witness the conversion of organization studies into something resembling a post-positivistic biosocial science that will provide an essential intellectual aide to policy elites attempting to develop solutions to '(super) wicked problems' (Conklin 2005; Ferlie et al. 2013).

We asked for an avoidance of a situation wherein the discipline was succumbing to voices calling for intellectual closure and control around a new orthodoxy. Studies of organization and organizing should be able to draw on as wide a range of analytical, theoretical, and methodological resources as possible, in order to comprehend the current state of the ways in which the world is organized. This may well involve a consideration of elements that are presently deemed to be unthinkable. Yet, they are true alternatives to all that have open minds. But the opening of minds to alternatives is not easy. Huge vested interests exist to maintain the status quo within conventional Organization Theory, whether it is to restrain feminist theorizing (Calas and Smircich 2019; Bell et al. 2019) or post-colonial thought (Frenkel and Shenhav 2006; Nkomo 2011; Jack et al. 2011). The hegemons will not surrender without a fight.

Alternative Forms of Organizing Requiring a Struggle

Reversing the usual structures of power would be nice. We (assuming you, dear reader, are one of 'us') might begin by seeking to reorganize the university, in Britain and elsewhere. This may be seen as a very provincial move but one has to start somewhere perhaps and where better than one's own organization. The history of the British university is in need of an organizational analysis itself. I have worked with people whose reputation for analytical skills in marketing and systems thinking was international, but they did not know the first thing about their own organizations. For the sea in which we swim is the last thing we theorize. Helpfully, Shattock (2000) provided a brief history of the development of the British university which has multiple threads to it. It is essential reading for anyone interested in the nature of their own organizations! Put crudely, regional business men (for they were men) often lay behind the sponsorship of provincial universities, seeing them in the line of Germanic thinking, started by Humboldt, to be centres of, and for, industrial research and teaching (Nyborn 2007). They were meant to be servants of industrial development. These sponsors such as the Armstrongs, the Wills, and the Boots families exercised considerable influence in how the university in their region developed. Only in the Post-War period of student expansion, beginning in the early 1950s, did Senates start to exercise more power than the families of the Founders and local 'worthies'. Vice-Chancellors saw themselves, perhaps, as academics and as being *primum inter pares*, and certainly not as enduring managers of a business. Under the Thatcher administration, where academics in the social sciences, in particular, were seen as problematic 'lefties' and as building centres of anti-government sentiment, legislation was brought into being that placed University Councils in a much more important position than Senates. Whilst the influence of the old families no longer held the level of pre-War sway that they once had, local businessmen and women were now placed back in control of the institutions. The academics represented by 'their' Senates, were no longer calling the shots. Councils did. These Councils (and their synonyms) started to employ, as Vice-Chancellors, people who looked more and more like themselves, and who employed methods more and more like local businesses. Thus, the period 1950–1985 looks like a time when many universities were organized in ways which had a distribution of power that allowed academics a role in running the institution. A return to those days would be welcome. We must note in passing, that in Oxford and Cambridge those days have not yet gone and the 'democratic' nature of these universities remains something to aspire to for most of us.

Outside the immediate world of universities, where the reader might start to imagine the scale of problems in bringing about a modicum of organizational transformation, let us imagine the possibilities that exist and the problems there might be in bringing about real change (Parker 2008; Parker et al. 2014). The journal *Ephemera* (Emma Jeanes et al. 2015), where one can find much material dealing with alternative ways of envisaging the social world, advertised a colloquium on alternative forms of organizing thus:

> The New Economics Foundation calls for a "Great Transition" (Ryan-Collins et al. 2009), in order to develop a fundamentally new economy based on sustainability, equality and stability. Scott-Cato and Hillier (2010) and Gibson-Graham (2006, 2008) argue that this will take place in the spaces left by current institutions through micropolitical processes which focus on a critical emancipation towards alternative systems. There has been work on alternative organization (Parker et al. 2014), imagining alternatives (Wright et al. 2013), and insights from counter-cultural forms of economy and organization (Parker 2011). These could suggest how already existing alternatives in the here and now might begin to unlock 'the potential for a range of diverse possibilities beyond capitalism' (Wilson 2013, p. 720).

They go on to say

> Pinning down what is meant by alternative, and the significance of alternative organization is a work in progress. Gibson-Graham et al. (2013) argue that the very label 'alternative' marginalizes non-dominant ways of organizing such that their credibility can be questioned. At the same time, being perceived as alternative could be part of an identity project of 'being minority' in which 'becoming mainstream' undermines and devalues its counter-cultural, – economic and – political status. However, for many, these alternatives enable experimentation in the politics of the possible, in order to seek a fundamentally changed society (Chatterton 2010).

This text raises the question of why use the term 'alternative' at all. Is it not a dangerous label to utilise in one's writing? I accept that it is, but from my position, any view of Organization Theory and its possibilities and problems have always faced questions of credibility. One cannot escape the fact that in a struggle, any struggle, the opposition will use whatever labels and terms and abusive suggestions that they can in order to undermine their opponents. This is part of the set of skills in rhetoric that British public schools teach their pupils from the outset (Peel et al. 2000). 'Being minority' is also a position with which people like me are not unhappy. Look around you in the university context today are there will be huge swathes of colleagues that one would not want to work with. They may well be looking at you with precisely the same feelings. Be glad if there is a handful, or even one or two, with whom discourse and friendship is a real pleasure.

We cannot hope to begin to address all the options that exist for alternative ways of organizing our lives. As I have said above, there is 10,000 years of human organizing to get to grips with. Focussing very carefully and specifically then, we might consider the work of Hardt and Negri (2000), or of Derrida, for example, which take anti-capitalist forms (Deutscher 1998; Abbinnett 2007). In *The End of Capitalism?* Gibson-Graham (1996, p. 3) argue that the very idea of a non-capitalist economy takes the shape of an unlikelihood or even an impossibility:

> It becomes difficult to entertain a vision of the prevalence and vitality of noncapitalist economic forms, or of daily or partial replacements of capitalism by noncapitalist economic practices, or of capitalist retreats and reversals. In this sense, 'capitalist hegemony' operates not only as a constituent of, but also a brake upon, the anticapitalist imagination.

And, to be sure, this metaphorical brake constrains conventional Organization Theory too. So, our question in the last Chapter of this book is 'what might be found on the 9 metres of the wall that have been ignored for so long by our mindless concentration upon the 1 metre that remains visible because only what is to be found there is alleged to be viable'? Put simply, what has the anti-capitalist imagination to offer the readers of this book (Hassard et al. 2007; Hassard and Pym 2012)?

Helpfully, Gibson-Graham (1996, p. 5) argue that what we should be interested in is the process of 'unearthing, of bringing to light images and habits of understanding that constitute "hegemonic capitalism"'. My metaphor of choice, of course, is not unrelated to theirs. It is of gently displacing the camouflage that lies over the organized world in order to see what lies beneath. Within this camouflaged world, we are told that 'there is no alternative' to what we have today. 'Market forces' are often introduced to say one cannot go against what is happening 'in the system' and draw a veil over other ways of thought and action. Alternative ways of doing things are labelled, using discourses from political and economic sciences, as 'against the social contract, unrealistic, threatening representative democracy, ludicrous, impossible, hugely expensive, inefficient' and so on. The lexicon of terms used *against* historically based ways of organizing is enormous, save when they justify the current imbalances within the world. History is a resource that conservatives draw upon constantly. Perhaps we can too. The constraints on trying something radically 'new' (especially if it has been tried centuries before) are enormous, and this must be recognized. Historians are incredibly valuable in reminding us of deep time, but their prejudices are crucial in understanding their 'takes' on what has happened and why. Many are essentially very conservative and bring this attitude to their understanding of what is possible and what is not. One has to choose one's history and historians very carefully.

Against the Whiggish history of royalty, warriors, wars, and Prime Ministers, we need to place matriarchal tribes where women are in control of the economy, the polity, and civil society. We have to understand anarchist communes where huge efforts are made not to create hierarchical rankings of the membership; co-operatives, syndicalist based groupings, and a-cephalous groupings are worthy of analysis where no one is obviously the 'leader'. The cartoon, so typical of 1950s America, where the bipedal alien lands in the New Mexican desert and says (in English) 'take me to your leader' is a trope that still dominates. 'Leadership' is a concept in the twenty-first century that really needs exploding into its component parts, for it is such a block to change (Chhokar et al. 2007). To undertake this task, the 'followership' may need riots and rebellions, worker takeovers or social movements. Across the globe these methods of resistance are still in use. Each of these, however, are threatened by police and military action as soon as they are planned, never mind put into action. Warrior clans such as the Spartans or the Mafia or other machismo-based systems like the Hell's Angel bikers offer some insights into how to organize differently and illegally.

Immediately, the reader may say *these* are not social forms we wish to emulate. I understand that, but the point is not to look only for something utopian that one can mimic (Reedy 2002). It is to find what problems one might encounter in developing alternatives. To build, one needs to know what architectures, including masculinist violence, lie hidden in wait within the edifice. Meanwhile, outside of the factory and office based world that we tend to inhabit, the ways of organizing adopted by nomadic peoples; or perhaps living a life based on *Ubuntu*; the farm conceived of widely with the eyes of a peasant; the village and hamlet far from the gaze of an urban and suburban sprawl; the high-rise housing development and the favella residing both inside and outside the world's mega-cities; the medieval Household marking, with its capital 'H', its centrality to both subsistence production and to profit-based activity; the Edwardian garden village, the Georgian ship at sea; and a long list besides. I invite the reader to read more.

What could we learn from understanding the past and the present, the far and the near, the possible and the allegedly impossible? It is finding a time and a place, perhaps, to open our eyes and our ears, and think outside the boxed hedges and lines of espaliers that the 'discipline' places around us. The re-wilding of Organization Theory is overdue (Carolan 2015). Let us push on past the constraints of the haw-haw and see what lies beyond, even if it is extremely dangerous. The edge is surely there to be explored, even if we fall off it.

8 The Corporeal and the Corporate

Sites of Contested Ethics

This is a very brief concluding chapter to reiterate (if I must) the importance to Organization Theory of personal politics and of where one stands on issues that some might see only through the lens of pragmatism and what is alleged to be possible and practical. First, are organizations only about the exercise of power, the maintenance of the status quo for those in control, and the consequences for the personal life of those enrolled in senior (and junior) positions?

Our *bodies*, though we might not notice, are first in line for this exercise of organizational power upon them (Dale 2003; Thanem 2001, 2011; Hassard 2003; Rose et al. 2006). The importance of embodiment has been recognized because of the ways in which 'the body' has been presented in some areas as a fixed, material entity without agency of its own. The conceptual separation of the mind from the body, in which sentient beings have bodies merely to carry the mind around, is a perspective drawn from Descartes. But the recognition, in feminist studies, of the body and of its impact in organizational life has led to the body being seen as of equal importance to the mind (Williams and Mills 2019). Merleau-Ponty (1989, p. 3 quoted in Crossley 1995) said that 'the perceiving mind is an incarnated mind' putting this point very succinctly. It is an important move then to see the body not as fixed meat but as a something constantly in transition and constantly mobile. This is what the notion of 'embodiment' seeks to achieve. Dale's 2001 text on *Anatomising Embodiment and Organization Theory* shows the relevance of embodiment to Organization Theory because it reveals the politics of the body, the specificity of embodiment and not a single universalized notion of one body, and most importantly, the lived nature of embodiment as a phenomenological issue. The body (indeed, your body) then is both personal and political (Thanem 2004).

Turning now to the body politic. According to many commentators on the political Left, organizational life gives rise to the 'iron law of oligarchy' whereby those that find themselves in positions of power in the

DOI: 10.4324/9781003150503-8

organizational world seek to hang on to it, by almost any means possible. They spend their time maintaining their political grip on the machinery of power for their own purposes, not for those of their supporters and users. The bureaucratic imperative is also an issue for critics of what organizations do. Everything becomes seen as controllable within the machinery, by using established ways and traditional techniques. The pyramid is a monolith. Everything that arises in a novel form is subjected to old forms of understanding. The organization becomes the centre of technological and administrative conservatism.

Third, the organization attracts and even demands that its employees become 'organization man' and 'organization woman' (Whyte 2013), whose primary interests in life should be the corporation and its demands (Burrell and Dale 2014). These are diminished human beings whose focus becomes self-orientated within the collective, as they seek out only contributions to their perceived individual career. Of course, there are many other versions of what organizations do to, and with us, but so too are there voices that argue what organizations might do to *help* our lives.

The coordination of human effort working in the same direction can achieve much of human benefit. One need not be a 'utopian' to believe that in some places at some times, organizations offer ways in which the demonstrable 'good' for individuals can be achieved by the efforts of many. They are collective expressions of shared activity that have legitimacy and widespread respect. In the UK, there is huge support for the National Health Service, despite all its difficulties of sheer size, innumerable change programmes masquerading as 'reforms', and problems in recruitment to highly-stressed jobs. The BBC is less trusted today than it was for some degree of objectivity but the state-orientated bias, which it now clearly evinces, is rightly being challenged as a viewpoint of concern. Similarly, British universities were once seen as bastions of academic values that allowed free discussion in proper arenas for debate. The oft-used phrase 'the envy of the world' is a huge exaggeration, of course, but it was a system that had some strengths. This image too is somewhat tarnished by the reality of attacks upon staff, their working conditions, and reward systems within contemporary academe.

The voluntary sector is often seen as containing good exemplars of positivity wherein volunteers make the lives of their clients more bearable. Hi-tech companies might be seen as offering exciting jobs to highly trained people in what must be models of good jobs. Students flock to apply for such employment. Today, however, the promise of 'green', 'ethical' firms often turns out to be motivated by the search for the camouflage provided by 'greenwash'. But there are also alternatives to 'good' jobs as perceived in this somewhat limited way. There are some jobs that do 'good'. National crises throw up the importance of such activities that have previously been underestimated for their significance.

As was argued earlier, the military is often a place where organizational issues come to the fore in stark form. The RAF in 1940 played a considerable role in holding back Nazi forces, represented at the time through the Luftwaffe during the Battle of Britain. The Luftwaffe and the RAF were organized differently, especially on the dimension of centralization and decentralization (Raffel 2021), and after a time it became possible to see what were the different consequences of these separate organizational forms upon performance and outcome. Choices are available. And sometimes they are crucial. Similarly, perhaps, the organizational form adopted by the Zapitistas in Mexico show the possibilities for political life of acting and thinking differently (Castells et al. 1995). For a real embracing of ethics, as we might seek to understand them, one must look elsewhere in the organized world (Jones et al. 2005). *Ubuntu*, for example, challenges our Western worldview (Nansubuga and Munene 2019; Gaim and Clegg 2021) and is offered to us as another 'episteme'. Derived from Southern Africa, the greeting of one member of the society to another is 'I see you'. That is, your existence is recognized by the Other. Everyone becomes a person of note, worthy of recognition. This cannot be said to be true across the organizational world of the West (Jones et al. 2005).

Due to internal and external critiques of their functioning, organizations in the twenty-first century had found that their high visibility (often deliberately sought by their marketing executives) may well play a part in their downfall. The international and national press contains weekly discussions of corporate scandals and of corruption, for example, in Big Pharma and Big Energy and in Big Science as, *inter alia*, the public's data are lost and the privacy of citizens, clients, customers, and consumers are all compromised (Magill and Prybil 2004; Herschel and Miori 2017). The large organizations in this decade are enmired and besmirched, as old forms of regime maintenance are shown to be unable to deal with public scrutiny, especially via social media, where everyone seems to think their opinion actually matters.

In the face of this intense gaze, not from regulators whose performance is often desperately poor (Levine 2010), but from the 'public' in its vox populi mode, organizations have sought to camouflage themselves, often by hiding in plain sight. In some senses, the 'Age of the Robber Barons' (a title that re-appears periodically over time; Burbach et al. 2001) seems to have returned. And a good move for these plutocrats appears to be a retreat behind the thick castle walls of Xanadu and *Citizen Kane* obscurity. For, just as their success subsequently has brought failure, their visibility has subsequently encouraged hiding. In large measure, the organized world of 50 years ago with careers for life, a pyramidal structure, and a paper-based system of record keeping has 'disappeared' from view. But because such elements have retreated (in some measure) does not mean that the organization itself has become dis-eased or deceased. Hauntology implies that it has not gone away (Fisher 2012). It is hidden by layers of masking tape that offer up the real task for an edgy Organization Theory, fit for the foreseeable future. This difficult enterprise would be the revealing, the removal, and the analysis of the camouflage and what lies concealed beneath it. The vectors of concern beneath the occlusion should be organizational *shape, speed, and direction.* But by being investigative about these dimensions, paraethical researchers (McLeod et al. 2016; Herschel and Miori 2017; Magill and Prybil 2004) will carry many risks of which one needs to be fully aware (see the career of CW Mills: 2001) at the outset. But for me in 2022, and happily freed from the concerns of career, the way forward for Organization Theory is to grasp, for a little while and in a few places, that *the task is the mask.*

References

Abbinnett, R., 2007. Untimely agitations: Derrida, Klein and Hardt & Negri on the idea of anti-capitalism. *Journal for Cultural Research*, *11*(1), pp.41–56.

Abbott, J. and Bakan, J., 2020. *The new corporation: The unfortunately necessary sequel*. Telefilm Canada.

Abolafia, M.Y., Dodge, J.E. and Jackson, S.K., 2014. Clifford Geertz and the interpretation of organizations. In P. Adler, P. du Gay, G. Morgan and M. Reed, eds., *The Oxford handbook of sociology, social theory, and organization studies: Contemporary currents* (pp.346–369). Oxford University Press.

Abreu-Pederzini, G.D. and Suárez-Barraza, M.F., 2020. Just let us be: Domination, the postcolonial condition, and the global field of business schools. *Academy of Management Learning & Education*, *19*(1), pp.40–58.

Ackroyd, S., 2010. Critical realism, organization theory, methodology, and the emerging science of reconfiguration. In P. Koslowski, ed., *Elements of a philosophy of management and organization* (pp.47–77). Springer.

Ackroyd, S. and Fleetwood, S., 2005. *Critical realist applications in organisation and management studies*. Routledge.

Ackroyd, S. and Thompson, P., 2016. *Organizational misbehaviour*. Edward Elgar Publishing Limited.

Adler, P.S., Du Gay, P., Morgan, G. and Reed, M.I., eds., 2014. *The Oxford handbook of sociology, social theory, and organization studies: Contemporary currents*. Oxford Handbooks.

Adorno, T.W. and Horkheimer, M., 1997. *Dialectic of enlightenment*. Verso.

Adubato, S., 2011. Blackwater: Changing your name doesn't fix your reputation. In *You are the brand* (pp.105–108). Rutgers University Press.

Aglietta, M., 2000. *A theory of capitalist regulation: The US experience*. Verso.

Agrast, M.D., Bučar, B., Galič, A., Kerševan, E., Knez, R., Kraljić, S., Strban, G. and Tičar, L., 2013. *The world justice project rule of law index: 2012–2013*. Univerza v Mariboru, Pravna fakulteta.

Akram-Lodhi, A.H. and Kay, C., 2010. Surveying the agrarian question (part 2): Current debates and beyond. *The Journal of Peasant Studies*, *37*(2), pp.255–284.

Albrow, M., 1970. *Bureaucracy*. Macmillan International Higher Education.

Aldrich, H., 1988. Paradigm warriors: Donaldson versus the critics of organization theory. *Organization Studies*, *9*(1), pp.19–25.

Alon, I., Apriliyanti, I.D. and Parodi, M.C.H., 2020. A systematic review of international franchising. *Multinational Business Review*, *29*(1), pp.43–69.

Alvarado, J., 2009. Fair trade in Mexico and abroad: An alternative to the Walmartopia? *Journal of Business Ethics*, *88*(2), pp.301–317.

Alvesson, M., Bridgman, T. and Willmott, H., 2011. *The Oxford handbook of critical management studies*. Oxford University Press.

Amin, A., ed., 2011. *Post-Fordism: A reader*. John Wiley & Sons.

Anand, V., Rosen, C.C. and Franklin, D., 2014. Capturing value through secrecy: A process-oriented model of secret keeping in organizations. *Academy of Management Proceedings*, *2014*(1), pp.171–121.

Argyriades, D., 2010. From bureaucracy to debureaucratization? *Public Organization Review*, *10*(3), pp.275–297.

Bakhtin, M., 1975. *The dialogic imagination*. Manchester University Press.

Ball, K. and McLeod, T., eds., 2014. *Towards a political economy of surveillance*. Routledge.

Barad, K., 2003. Posthumanist performativity: Toward an understanding of how matter comes to matter. *Signs: Journal of Women in Culture and Society*, *28*(3), pp.801–831.

Barad, K., 2007. *Meeting the universe halfway: Quantum physics and the entanglement of matter and meaning*. Duke University Press.

Barad, K., 2007, July. Meeting the universe halfway. In *Meeting the universe halfway*. Duke University Press.

Barley, S.R., 1983. Semiotics and the study of occupational and organizational cultures. *Administrative Science Quarterly*, *28*(3), pp.393–413.

Basbøll, T., 2010. Multiple failures of scholarship: Karl Weick and the Mann Gulch Disaster. In P. Armstrong and G. Lightfoot, eds., *The leading journal in the field: Destabilizing authority in the social sciences of management* (pp.85–102). Mayfly Press.

Bauman, Z., 1990. Modernity and ambivalence. *Theory, Culture & Society*, *7*(2–3), pp.143–169.

Bauman, Z., 2000. *Modernity and the holocaust*. Cornell University Press.

Bell, E., Meriläinen, S., Taylor, S. and Tienari, J., 2019. Time's up! Feminist theory and activism meets organization studies. *Human Relations*, *72*(1), pp.4–22.

Beneker, J., 2011. The crossing of the rubicon and the outbreak of civil war in Cicero, Lucan, Plutarch, and Suetonius. *Phoenix*, *65*(1/2), pp.74–99.

Bhatt, E.R., 2006. *We are poor but so many: The story of self-employed women in India*. Oxford University Press.

Bhatt, E.R. and Jhabvala, R., 2004. The idea of work. *Economic and Political Weekly*, November 27, pp.5133–5140.

Bhatt, E. and Jhabvala, R., 2012. *Ahmedabad: A history of SEWA*. Navajivan Publishing.

Blackburn, R.A., Hart, M., Smallbone, D., Kitching, J., Eadson, W. and Bannon, K., 2005. *Analysis of the impact of the tax system on the cash flow of small businesses: A report for HM Revenue and Customs (HMRC)*. Her Majesty's Customs and Revenue Office.

Bogue, R., 2008. *Deleuze and Guattari*. Routledge.

Boje, D.M., 2008. *Storytelling organizations*. Sage.

Boje, D.M. and Smith, R., 2016. Re-storying and visualizing the changing entrepreneurial identities of Bill Gates and Richard Branson. *Culture and Organization*, *16*(4), pp.307–331.

Boje, D.M., 2019. *Storytelling in the global age: There is no planet B* (Vol. 1). World Scientific.

Borras Jr., S.M., 2009. Agrarian change and peasant studies: Changes, continuities and challenges–an introduction. *The Journal of Peasant Studies*, *36*(1), pp.5–31.

Boyd, C., 1990. The responsibility of individuals for a company disaster: The case of the Zeebrugge car ferry. In G. Moorhead and R.W. Griffin, eds., *People in corporations* (pp.139–148). Springer.

Boyer, R., 2005. How and why capitalisms differ. *Economy and Society*, *34*(4), pp.509–557.

Branson, R., 2011. *Losing my virginity*. Random House.

Brignall, M., 2021. Quarter of workers plan move to new job in next six months. *Guardian*. November 1, p.31.

Bruce, W., 2000. Breaking the psychological contract: An act of anti-ethics. *Global Virtue Ethics Review*, *2*(2), pp.134–145.

Bryman, A., 1999. The disneyization of society. *The Sociological Review*, *47*(1), pp.25–47.

Buchanan, D. and Bryman, A., eds., 2009. *The Sage handbook of organizational research methods*. Sage.

Bulley, D. and Brassett, J., 2021. Everyday ethics of the global event: Grenfell Tower and the politics of responsibility. *Globalizations*, *18*(4), pp.551–567.

Burbach, R., Robinson, B., Jeffries, F. and Robinson, W.I., 2001. *Globalization and postmodern politics: From Zapatistas to high-tech robber barons*. Pluto Press.

Burrell, G., 1997. *Pandemonium: Towards a retro-organization theory*. Sage.

Burrell, G., 2018. Chaos: The unspoken other to organization theory. In T. Peleton, H. Gaggiotti and P. Case (eds.), *Origins of organizing* (Chapter 1, pp.3–27). Edward Elgar.

Burrell, G., 2020. W(h)ither the peasantry in the work of the academy? *Academy of Management Discoveries*, *6*(2), pp.1–2.

Burrell, G. and Dale, K., 2014. Space and organization studies. In P. Adler, P. Du Gay, G. Morgan and M. Reed (eds.), *The Oxford handbook of sociology, social theory, and organization studies* (pp.694–708). Oxford University Press.

Burrell, G. and Morgan, G., 2017. *Sociological paradigms and organisational analysis: Elements of the sociology of corporate life*. Routledge.

Byres, T.J., 1973. The journal of peasant studies: Its origins and some reflections on the first twenty years. In H. Bernstein, T. Brass, and T.J. Byres, with E. Lahiff and G. Peace (eds.), *The journal of peasant studies: A twenty volume index 1973–1993* (pp.1–12). Frank Cass.

Butler, S., 2021. Number of gig economy workers has more than doubled in five years. *The Guardian*, November 5, p.38.

Cairns, G., 2007. Postcard from Chittagong: Wish you were here? *Critical Perspectives on International Business*, *3*(3), pp.266–279.

Calás, M.B. and Smircich, L., 2006. 1.8 From the 'woman's point of view' ten years later: Towards a feminist organization studies. In *The Sage handbook of organization studies* (pp. 284–301). Sage.

Calás, M.B. and Smircich, L., 2019. A heart felt remembrance: Some of the ways we knew Joan Acker. *Gender, Work & Organization, 26*(12), pp.1694–1701.

Callaci, B., 2021. Control without responsibility: The legal creation of franchising, 1960–1980. *Enterprise & Society, 22*(1), pp.156–182.

Carolan, M., 2015. Re-wilding food systems: Visceralities, utopias, pragmatism, and practice. In P.V. Stock, M. Carolan and C. Rosin (eds.), *Food utopias: Reimagining citizenship, ethics and community* (pp. 126–139). Routledge.

Carolei, D., 2018. How is Oxfam being held accountable over the Haiti scandal? *Democratic Audit Blog.*

Case, P., 1999. Remember re-engineering? The rhetorical appeal of a managerial salvation device. *Journal of Management Studies, 36*(4), pp.419–441.

Case, P. and Gosling, J., 2010. The spiritual organization: Critical reflections on the instrumentality of workplace spirituality. *Journal of Management, Spirituality and Religion, 7*(4), pp.257–282.

Casey, C., 2002. *Critical analysis of organizations: Theory, practice, revitalization.* Sage.

Castells, M., Yazawa, S. and Kiselyova, E., 1995. Insurgents against the global order: A comparative analysis of the Zapatistas in Mexico, the American militia and Japan's AUM Shinrikyo. *Berkeley Journal of Sociology, 40*, pp.21–59.

Chatterton, P., 2010. So what does it mean to be anti-capitalist? Conversations with activists from urban social centres. *Urban Studies, 47*(6), pp.1205–1224.

Chernick, H., ed., 2005. *Resilient city: The economic impact of 9/11.* Russell Sage Foundation.

Chernykh, L. and Mityakov, S., 2017. Offshore schemes and tax evasion: The role of banks. *Journal of Financial Economics, 126*(3), pp.516–542.

Chhokar, J.S., Brodbeck, F.C. and House, R.J., eds., 2007. *Culture and leadership across the world: The GLOBE book of in-depth studies of 25 societies.* Routledge.

Citations Needed, 2021. Episode 145: How real estate-curated 'mom & pop landlord' sob stories are used to gut tenant protections. September 29, 2021.

Clegg, S., 1994. Weber and Foucault: Social theory for the study of organizations. *Organization, 1*(1), pp.149–178.

Clegg, S., 2010. The state, power, and agency: Missing in action in institutional theory? *Journal of Management Inquiry, 19*(1), pp.4–13.

Clegg, S., 2017. The East India company: The first modern multinational? In C. Dörrenbächer and M. Geppert, eds., *Multinational corporations and organization theory: Post millennium perspectives.* Emerald Publishing Limited, in *Research in the Sociology of Organizations, 49*, pp.43–67.

Clegg, S. and Dunkerley, D., 1980. *Organisations, class and control.* Routledge & Kegan Paul.

Clegg, S.R., Hardy, C. and Nord, W.R., 1996. *Handbook of organization studies.* Sage.

Clegg, S.R., Kornberger, M. and Rhodes, C., 2005. Learning/becoming/organizing. *Organization, 12*(2), pp.147–167.

Collinson, D.L., 2003. Identities and insecurities: Selves at work. *Organization*, *10*(3), pp.527–547.

Conklin, J., 2005. *Dialogue mapping: Building shared understanding of wicked problems*. John Wiley & Sons, Inc.

Contu, A., 2008. Decaf resistance: On misbehavior, cynicism, and desire in liberal workplaces. *Management Communication Quarterly*, *21*(3), pp.364–379.

Contu, A., 2009. Critical management education. In M. Alvesson, T. Bridgman and H. Willmott, eds., *The Oxford handbook of critical management studies* (pp.536–550). Oxford University Press.

Cooke, B., 2003. The denial of slavery in management studies. *Journal of Management Studies*, *40*(8), pp.1895–1918.

Cooper, R. and Fox, S., 1990. The 'texture'of organizing. *Journal of Management Studies*, *27*(6), pp.575–582.

Cooper, G., 2019. #Aid too? The 2018 humanitarian scandals in Oxfam GB and save the children UK. In H. Tumber and S. Waisbord, eds., *The Routledge companion to media and scandal* (pp.342–353). Routledge.

Cooper, R., 2015. Organization/disorganization. In G. Burrell and M. Parker, eds., *For Robert Cooper* (pp.87–123). Routledge.

Cornelissen, J.P., 2004. What are we playing at? Theatre, organization, and the use of metaphor. *Organization Studies*, *25*(5), pp.705–726.

Cornelissen, J.P., Oswick, C., Thøger Christensen, L. and Phillips, N., 2008. Metaphor in organizational research: Context, modalities and implications for research—Introduction. *Organization Studies*, *29*(1), pp.7–22.

Crossley, N., 1995. Merleau-Ponty, the elusive body and carnal sociology. *Body & Society*, *1*(1), pp.43–63.

Cruver, B., 2003. *Enron: Anatomy of greed: The unshredded truth from an Enron insider*. Random House.

Cummings, S. and Thanem, T., 2002. Essai: The ghost in the organism. *Organization Studies*, *23*(5), pp.817–839.

Cunliffe, A.L., 2008. *Organization theory*. Sage.

Cunliffe, A.L. and Luhman, J.T., 2012. *Key concepts in organization theory*. Sage.

Cunliffe, A.L., Luhman, J.T. and Boje, D.M., 2004. Narrative temporality: Implications for organizational research. *Organization Studies*, *25*(2), pp.261–286.

Czarniawska, B., 1997. *Narrating the organization: Dramas of institutional identity*. University of Chicago Press.

Czarniawska, B., 2008. *The theory of organizing*. Sage.

Czarniawska, B., Miscione, G., Raviola, E., Alcadipani da Silveira, R. and Tarim, E., 2021. *Call for papers: Organizing outside organizations*. Sage.

Dacin, M., Goodstein, J. and Richard Scott, W., 2002. Institutional theory and institutional change: Introduction to the special research forum. *Academy of Management Journal*, *45*(1), pp.45–56.

Daft, R.L., Murphy, J. and Willmott, H., 2010. *Organization theory and design*. Cengage Learning. Inc.

Daft, R.L., Murphy, J. and Willmott, H., 2017. *Organization theory & design: An international perspective*. Cengage Learning.

Dale, E., 1959. Some foundations of organization theory. *California Management Review*, *2*(1), pp.71–84.

Dale, K., 2000. *Anatomising embodiment and organisation theory.* Springer.

Dale, K., 2005. Building a social materiality: Spatial and embodied politics in organizational control. *Organization*, *12*(5), pp.649–678.

Dale, K., 2012. The employee as 'dish of the day': The ethics of the consuming/consumed self in human resource management. *Journal of Business Ethics*, *111*(1), pp.13–24.

Dale, K. and Burrell, G., 2003. An-aesthetics and architecture. In A. Carr and P. Hancock, eds., *Art and aesthetics at work* (pp.155–173). Palgrave Macmillan.

Dale, K. and Burrell, G., 2010. Disturbing structure, reading the ruins. *Culture and Organization*, *17*(2), pp.107–121.

Dale, K. and Burrell, G., 2013. Being occupied: An embodied re-reading of organizational wellness. *Organization*, *21*(2), pp.159–177.

Dale, K. and Burrell, G., 2015. Leadership and space in 3D: Distance, dissent and disembodiment in the case of a new academic building. In A. Ropo, P. Salovaara, E. Sauer and D. De Paoli, eds., *Leadership in spaces and places* (pp.217–241). Edward Elgar Publishing.

Dale, K. and Latham, Y., 2015. Ethics and entangled embodiment: Bodies–materialities–organization. *Organization*, *22*(2), pp.166–182.

Davies, W., 2015. *The happiness industry: How the government and big business sold us well-being.* Verso Books.

Davis, G.F., 2015. Celebrating organization theory: The after-party. *Journal of Management Studies*, *52*(2), pp.309–319.

Davis, A. and Williams, K., 2017. Introduction: Elites and power after financialization. *Theory, Culture & Society*, *34*(5–6), pp.3–26.

Davis, G.F. and Marquis, C., 2005. Prospects for organization theory in the early twenty-first century: Institutional fields and mechanisms. *Organization Science*, *16*(4), pp.332–343.

DeArmitt, P., 2013. *The right to narcissism.* Fordham University Press.

Deleuze, G. and Guattari, F., 1974. *Anti-Oedipus: Capitalism and schizophrenia.* Penguin.

Deleuze, G. and Guattari, F., 1988. *A thousand plateaus: Capitalism and schizophrenia.* Bloomsbury Publishing.

Deutscher, P., 1998. Mourning the other, cultural cannibalism, and the politics of friendship (Jacques Derrida and Luce Irigaray). *Differences: A Journal of Feminist Cultural Studies*, *10*(3), pp.159–184.

DiMaggio, P.J. and Powell, W.W., 1991. *The iron cage revisited.* University of Chicago Press.

DiMaggio, P.J. and Powell, W.W., 2000. The iron cage revisited; institutional isomorphism and collective rationality in organizational fields. In J. Baum and F. Dobbin, eds., *Economics meets sociology in strategic management* (pp.143–166). JAI Press.

Domagal, J., 2002. Keeping secrets: Student secret societies in historical context. *The Vermont Connection*, *23*(1), p.6.

Donaldson, L., 1988. In successful defence of organization theory: A routing of the critics. *Organization Studies*, 9(1), pp.28–32.

Donaldson, L., 1998. The myth of paradigm incommensurability in management studies: Comments by an integrationist. *Organization*, 5(2), pp.267–272.

Donaldson, L., 2003. Organization theory as a positive science. In H. Tsoukas and C. Knudsen, eds., *The Oxford handbook of organization theory* (pp.39–62). Oxford University Press.

Du Gay, P., 2000. *In praise of bureaucracy: Weber-organization-ethics*. Sage.

Du Gay, P., ed., 2005. *The values of bureaucracy*. OUP.

Du Gay, P., 2013. New spirits of public management...'Post-Bureaucracy.' In P. Du Gay & G. Morgan, eds., *New spirits of capitalism? Crises, justifications, and dynamics* (pp.274–293). Oxford University Press.

Dubos, R., 2017. *Social capital: Theory and research*. Routledge.

Duggan, J., Sherman, U., Carbery, R. and McDonnell, A., 2020. Algorithmic management and app-work in the gig economy: A research agenda for employment relations and HRM. *Human Resource Management Journal*, 30(1), pp.114–132.

Dundon, T. and Rafferty, A., 2018. The (potential) demise of HRM? *Human Resource Management Journal*, 28(3), pp.377–391.

Dwyer, G. and Hardy, C., 2016. We have not lived long enough: Sensemaking and learning from bushfire in Australia. *Management Learning*, 47(1), pp.45–64.

Engels, F., 1976. *The peasant war in Germany*. Routledge.

Epstein, G.A., ed., 2005. *Financialization and the world economy*. Edward Elgar Publishing.

Etzioni, A., 1960. New directions in the study of organizations and society (Note). *Social Research*, 27(1), p.223.

Fairclough, N., 2005. Peripheral vision: Discourse analysis in organization studies: The case for critical realism. *Organization Studies*, 26(6), pp.915–939.

Felstead, A. and Jewson, N., 2002. *In work, at home: Towards an understanding of homeworking*. Routledge.

Felstead, A., Jewson, N. and Walters, S., 2005. The shifting locations of work: New statistical evidence on the spaces and places of employment. *Work, Employment and Society*, 19(2), pp.415–431.

Ferlie, E., Fitzgerald, L., McGivern, G., Dopson, S., and Bennett, C., 2013. *Making wicked problems governable? The case of managed networks in health care*. OUP.

Ferguson, N., 2019. *The square and the tower: Networks and power, from the Freemasons to Facebook*. Penguin Books.

Fineman, S., Gabriel, Y. and Sims, D., 2009. *Organizing & organizations*. Sage.

Fisher, M., 2012. What is hauntology? *Film Quarterly*, 66(1), pp.16–24.

Fleming, P., 2014. When 'life itself' goes to work: Reviewing shifts in organizational life through the lens of biopower. *Human Relations*, 67(7), pp.875–901.

Fleming, P., 2017. The human capital hoax: Work, debt and insecurity in the era of Uberization. *Organization Studies*, 38(5), pp.691–709.

Fleming, P., 2020. Dark academia: Despair in the neoliberal business school. *Journal of Management Studies*, 57(6), pp.1305–1311.

Fleming, P., 2021. The Ghost University: Academe from the Ruins. *Emancipations: A Journal of Critical Social Analysis*, *1*(1), p.4.

Fleming, P. and Sturdy, A., 2009. "Just be yourself!": Towards neo-normative control in organisations? *Employee Relations*, *31*(6), pp.569–583.

Foss, N.J., 2007. The emerging knowledge governance approach: Challenges and characteristics. *Organization*, *14*(1), pp.29–52.

Foucault, M., 1985. Final interview. *Raritan*, *5*(1), pp.1–13.

Fournier, V. and Grey, C., 2000. At the critical moment: Conditions and prospects for critical management studies. *Human Relations*, *53*(1), pp.7–32.

Freedland, M., 2006. From the contract of employment to the personal work nexus. *Industrial Law Journal*, *35*(1), pp.1–29.

Freedman, L., 1982. The war of the Falkland Islands, 1982. *Foreign Affairs*, *61*(1), pp.196–210.

Frenkel, M. and Shenhav, Y., 2006. From binarism back to hybridity: A postcolonial reading of management and organization studies. *Organization Studies*, *27*(6), pp.855–876.

Friedman, A., 1990. Managerial strategies, activities, techniques and technology: Towards a complex theory of the labour process. In M. Alvesson and H. Willmott, eds., *Labour process theory* (pp.177–208). Palgrave Macmillan.

Frost, P., 1980. Toward a radical framework for practicing organization science. *Academy of Management Review*, *5*(4), pp.501–507.

Fukuyama, F., 2006. *The end of history and the last man*. Simon and Schuster.

Gabriel, Y., 1999. *Organizations in depth: The psychoanalysis of organizations*. Sage.

Gabriel, Y., 2015. Psychoanalysis and the study of organization. In *The Routledge companion to philosophy in organization studies* (pp.244–256). Routledge.

Gabriel, Y., 2019. Personal blog site.

Gaim, M. and Clegg, S., 2021. Paradox beyond East/West orthodoxy: The case of Ubuntu. In R. Bednarek, M.P.e Cunha, J. Schad and W.K. Smith (eds.), *Interdisciplinary dialogues on organizational paradox: Learning from belief and science*. Emerald Group Publishing.

Gabriel, Y., 2020. Kafka and the COVID-19 epidemic: Why the Sirens' silence is more deadly than their song. *Leadership*, *16*(3), pp.320–330.

Galbraith, J.K., 2008. *The predator state: How conservatives abandoned the free market and why liberals should too*. Simon and Schuster.

Gedajlovic, E., Yoshikawa, T. and Hashimoto, M., 2005. Ownership structure, investment behaviour and firm performance in Japanese manufacturing industries. *Organization Studies*, *26*(1), pp.7–35.

Geertz, C., 1973. *The interpretation of cultures*. Basic Books.

Geiger, D. and Antonacopoulou, E., 2009. Narratives and organizational dynamics: Exploring blind spots and organizational inertia. *The Journal of Applied Behavioral Science*, *45*(3), pp.411–436.

Gergen, K., 1991. *The saturated self: Dilemmas of identity in contemporary life*. Basic.

Gerth, H.H. and Mills, C.W., 1957 / 2014. *From Max Weber: Essays in sociology*. Routledge.

Ghoshal, S. and Westney, D.E., eds., 1993. *Organization theory and the multinational corporation*. Macmillan.

Giacalone, R.A. and Rosenfeld, P., 2013. *Impression management in the organization*. Psychology Press.

Gibson-Graham, J. K., 1996. *The end of capitalism*. Blackwell.

Gibson-Graham, J.K., 2006. Imagining and enacting a postcapitalist feminist economic politics. *Women's Studies Quarterly*, *34*(1/2), pp.72–78.

Gibson-Graham, J.K., 2008. Diverse economies: Performative practices for other worlds'. *Progress in Human Geography*, *32*(5), pp.613–632.

Gibson-Graham, J.K., Cameron, J. and Healy, S., 2013. *Take back the economy: An ethical guide for transforming our communities*. University of Minnesota Press.

Gillespie, K., 2015. *Elon Musk*. Weigl Publishers.

Goffman, E., 1972. The presentation of self to others. In *Symbolic interaction: A reader in social psychology* (pp.234–244). Alwyn and Bacon.

Goffman, E., 1978. *The presentation of self in everyday life*. Harmondsworth.

Gouvea, R., Montoya, M. and Walsh, S., 2013. How the corruption Quadruple Helix affects BRIC: A case study of corruption in big emerging economies. *Journal of Politics and Law*, *6*, p.1.

Graeber, D., 2014. *Bullshit jobs: The rise of pointless work, and what we can do about it*. Penguin.

Grant, D., Iedema, R. and Oswick, C., 2009. Discourse and critical management studies. In M. Alvesson, T. Bridgman and H. Willmott, eds., *The Oxford handbook of critical management studies* (pp.213–231). Oxford University Press.

Granter, E., McCann, L. and Boyle, M., 2015. Extreme work/normal work: Intensification, storytelling and hypermediation in the (re) construction of 'the New Normal'. *Organization*, *22*(4), pp.443–456.

Greenwood, R. and Hinings, C.R., 1996. Understanding radical organizational change: Bringing together the old and the new institutionalism. *Academy of Management Review*, *21*(4), pp.1022–1054.

Grey, C. and Willmott, H., eds., 2005. *Critical management studies: A reader*. Oxford University Press.

Griffith, J.A.G., 1977. *The politics of the judiciary*. Manchester University Press.

Guillen, M.F., 1994a. The age of eclecticsm: Current organizational trends and the evolution of managerial models. *MIT Sloan Management Review*, *36*(1), pp.75–87.

Guillén, M.F., 1994b. *Models of management: Work, authority, and organization in a comparative perspective*. University of Chicago Press.

Guillén, M.F., 2010. *The limits of convergence*. Princeton University Press.

Handy, J., 2009. 'Almost idiotic wretchedness': A long history of blaming peasants. *The Journal of Peasant Studies*, *36*(2), pp.325–344.

Harris, R., 2015. The changing nature of the workplace and the future of office space. *Journal of Property Investment & Finance*, *33*(5), pp.424–435.

Hardt, M. and Negri, A., 2000. *Empire*. Harvard University Press.

Hassard, J., Holliday, R. and Willmott, H., eds., 2000. *Body and organization*. Sage.

Hassard, J., Kelemen, M. and Cox, J.W., 2007. *Disorganization theory: Explorations in alternative organizational analysis*. Routledge.

Hassard, J. and Pym, D., eds., 2012. *The theory and philosophy of organizations: Critical issues and new perspectives*. Routledge.

Hatch, M.J. and Cunliffe, A.L., 2006. *Modern, symbolic, and postmodern perspectives*. Oxford University Press.

Hatch, M.J. and Weick, K.E., 1998. Critics' corner—critical resistance to the Jazz Metaphor. *Organization Science*, 9(5), pp.600–604.

Hatch, M.J. and Yanow, D., 2003. Organization theory as an interpretive science. In H. Tsoukas and C. Knudsen, eds., *The Oxford handbook of organization theory* (pp.39–62). Oxford University Press.

Hayes, C., 2008. *Popper, Hayek and the open society*. Routledge.

Heath, C. and Luff, P., 2000. *Technology in action*. Cambridge University Press.

Heckscher, C., 1994. Defining the post-bureaucratic type. In C. Heckscher and A. Donnellon (eds.), *The post-bureaucratic organization: New perspectives on organizational change* (pp.98–106). Sage.

Herschel, R. and Miori, V.M., 2017. Ethics & big data. *Technology in Society*, 49, pp.31–36.

Hickson, D.J., Hinings, C.R., McMillan, C.J. and Schwitter, J.P., 1974. The culture-free context of organization structure: A tri-national comparison. *Sociology*, 8(1), pp.59–80.

Hinings, B. and Meyer, R.E., 2018. *Starting points: Intellectual and institutional foundations of organization theory*. Cambridge University Press.

Hobsbawm, E.J., 1973. Peasants and politics. *The Journal of Peasant Studies*, 1(1), pp.3–22.

House of Commons Health and Social Care and Science and Technology Committees, 2021. Coronavirus: Lessons learned to date. September 21, 2021.

Hoy, F., Perrigot, R. and Terry, A., eds., 2017. *Handbook of research on franchising*. Edward Elgar Publishing.

Huxley, J., 1943. *TVA, adventure in planning*. RKP.

Ibrahim, A.M., Hassanain, M.A. and Al-Hammad, A.M., 2021. Maturity of workplace relocation: A systematic literature review from 1990 to 2020. *Facilities*, 39, pp.759–777.

Iedema, R., 2003. *Discourses of post-bureaucratic organization* (Vol. 5). John Benjamins Publishing.

Indicators, W.G., 2016. *Control of corruption index*. World Bank Policy Research Working Paper 4654, June, Washington, DC.

Introna, L.D., 2016. Algorithms, governance, and governmentality: On governing academic writing. *Science, Technology, & Human Values*, 41(1), pp.17–49.

Introna, L.D. and Nissenbaum, H., 2000. Shaping the web: Why the politics of search engines matters. *The Information Society*, 16(3), pp.169–185.

Irigaray, L., 2008. *Conversations*. Bloomsbury Publishing.

Jack, G., Westwood, R., Srinivas, N. and Sardar, Z., 2011. Deepening, broadening and re-asserting a postcolonial interrogative space in organization studies. *Organization*, 18(3), pp.275–302.

Jancsics, D., 2017. Offshoring at home? Domestic use of shell companies for corruption. *Public Integrity, 19*(1), pp.4–21.

Jeanes, E., Loacker, B., Sliwa, M. and Weiskopf, R., 2015. Mobilities in contemporary worlds of work and organizing. *Ephemera, 15*(4), p.705.

Jeffcutt, P., 1994. From interpretation to representation in organizational analysis: Postmodernism, ethnography and organizational symbolism. *Organization Studies, 15*(2), pp.241–274.

Jennings, P.D. and Greenwood, R., 2003. Constructing the iron cage: Institutional theory and enactment. In R. Westwood and S. Clegg, eds., *Debating organization: Point-counterpoint in organization studies* (pp.195–207). John Wiley & Sons.

Jessop, B., 2012. *The world market, variegated capitalism and the crisis of European integration* (pp.115–135). Routledge.

Jessop, B., 2013. Hollowing out the 'nation-state' and multi-level governance. In B. Jessop and P. Kennett, eds., *A handbook of comparative social policy* (pp.11–26), 2nd ed. Edward Elgar Publishing.

Jones, C., Parker, M. and Ten Bos, R., 2005. *For business ethics*. Routledge.

Jones, S., 2014. How to build an 'intrapreneurial' culture -an entrepreneurial culture within an organization. *Effective Executive, 17*(2), p.40.

Katz, C.J., 1992. Marx on the peasantry: Class in itself or class in struggle? *The Review of Politics, 54*(1), pp.50–71.

Kaufmann, D., Kraay, A. and Mastruzzi, M., 2010. The worldwide governance indicators: Methodology and analytical issues. *World Bank Policy Research Working Paper*, 5430.

Kitanaka, J., 2015. The rebirth of secrets and the new care of the self in depressed Japan. *Current Anthropology, 56*(S12), pp.S251–S262.

Klein, N., 2000. *No logo: Taking aim at the brand name bullies*. Flamingo.

Knights, D., 2009. Power at work in organizations. In M. Alvesson, T. Bridgman and H. Willmott, eds., *The Oxford handbook of critical management studies* (pp.144–165). Oxford University Press.

Knouse, S.B., Hill, V.D. and Hamilton, J.B., 2007. Curves in the high road: A historical analysis of the development of American business codes of ethics. *Journal of Management History, 13*(1), pp.94–107.

Komić, D., Marušić, S.L., and Marušić, A., 2015. Research integrity and research ethics in professional codes of ethics: Survey of terminology used by professional organizations across research disciplines. *PloS One, 10*(7), p.e0133662.

Kuhn, T.S., 1963. *The structure of scientific revolutions*. University of Chicago Press

Kuhn, T.S., 1970. *The structure of scientific revolutions 3*. University of Chicago Press.

Kuhn, T.S. and Hacking, I., 2012. *The structure of scientific revolutions: 50th anniversary edition*. University of Chicago Press.

Langley, A. and Tsoukas, H., 2010. Introducing perspectives on process organization studies. *Process, Sensemaking, and Organizing, 1*(9), pp.1–27.

Lapavitsas, C., 2011. Theorizing financialization. *Work, Employment and Society, 25*(4), pp.611–626.

88   *References*

Latour, B., 1990. On Actor-Network Theory. A few clarifications, plus more than a few complications. *Philosophia*, *25*(3), pp.47–64.

Latour, B., 2004. Why has critique run out of steam? From matters of fact to matters of concern. *Critical Inquiry*, *30*(2), pp.225–248.

Latour, B., 2017. On actor-network theory. A few clarifications, plus more than a few complications. *Philosophical Literary Journal Logos*, *27*(1), pp.173–197.

Law, J., 1984. On the methods of long-distance control: Vessels, navigation and the Portuguese route to India. *The Sociological Review*, *32*(1), pp.234–263.

Law, J. and Hassard, J., 1999. *Actor network theory and after*. Blackwell.

Ledeneva, A., 1998. *Russia's economy of favours: Blat, networking and informal exchange*. Cambridge University Press.

Ledeneva, A., 2000. *Continuity and change of blat practices in soviet and post-soviet Russia*. Macmillan.

Ledeneva, A., 2003. *Informal practices in changing societies: Comparing Chinese Guanxi and Russian Blat* (No. 45). UCL School of Slavonic and East European Studies (SSEES).

Ledeneva, A., 2008. Blat and Guanxi: Informal practices in Russia and China. *Comparative Studies in Society and History*, *50*(1), pp.118–144.

Ledeneva, A., ed., 2018. *The global encyclopaedia of informality, volume 1: Towards understanding of social and cultural complexity*. UCL Press.

Lencioni, P.M., 2015. *The truth about employee engagement: A fable about addressing the three root causes of job misery*. John Wiley & Sons.

Levine, R., 2010. An autopsy of the US financial system: Accident, suicide, or negligent homicide. *Journal of Financial Economic Policy*, *2*(3), pp.196–213.

Lewchuk, W., de Wolff, A., King, A. and Polanyi, M., 2006. The hidden costs of precarious employment: Health and the employment relationship. In *Precarious employment: Understanding labour market insecurity in Canada* (pp.141–162). WSIB Final Report. McMaster University.

Linstead, S. and Grafton-Small, R., 1992. On reading organizational culture. *Organization Studies*, *13*(3), pp.331–355.

Linstead, S. and Thanem, T., 2007. Multiplicity, virtuality and organization: The contribution of Gilles Deleuze. *Organization Studies*, *28*(10), pp.1483–1501.

Livingstone, D.N., 1987. Human acclimatization: perspectives on a contested field of inquiry in science, medicine and geography. *History of Science*, *25*(4), pp.359–394.

Livingstone, D.W., 1999. Beyond human capital theory: The underemployment problem. *International Journal of Contemporary Sociology*, *36*(2), pp.163–192.

Lounsbury, M. and Beckman, C.M., 2015. Celebrating organization theory. *Journal of Management Studies*, *52*(2), pp.288–308.

Love, T.R., 2018. *Indigenous organization studies: Exploring management, business and community*. Springer.

Löwy, M. and Löwy, M., 2000. From captain swing to pancho villa. Instances of peasant resistance in the historiography of Eric Hobsbawm. *Diogenes*, *48*(189), pp.3–10.

Lynch, M., 1985, republished 2017. *Art and artifact in laboratory science: A study of shop work and shop talk in a research laboratory*. Routledge.

Lyng, S., 1990. Edgework: A social psychological analysis of voluntary risk taking. *American Journal of Sociology*, *95*(4), pp.851–886.

Macfarlane, R., 2016. The secrets of the wood wide web. *The New Yorker*, *7*.

Macpherson, C.B., 2010. *The political theory of possessive individualism: Hobbes to Locke*. Clarendon Press.

Magill, G. and Prybil, L., 2004. Stewardship and integrity in health care: A role for organizational ethics. *Journal of Business Ethics*, *50*(3), pp.225–238.

March, J.G., 2005. Parochialism in the evolution of a research community: The case of organization studies. *Management and Organization Review*, *1*(1), pp.5–22.

Marsden, R., 2005. The politics of organizational analysis. In C. Grey and H. Willmott (eds.), *Critical management studies: A reader* (pp.132–164). Oxford University Press.

Martin, J., 2001. *Organizational culture: Mapping the terrain*. Sage.

Maynard, D.W. and Clayman, S.E., 1991. The diversity of ethnomethodology. *Annual Review of Sociology*, *17*(1), pp.385–418.

McCusker, R., 1999. Codes of ethics as corporate camouflage: An expression of desire, intent or deceit? *Journal of Financial Crime*, *7*(2), pp.104–146.

McFall, L. and Ossandón, J., 2014. What's new in the 'new, new economic sociology' and should organization studies care? In P. Adler, P. du Gay, G. Morgan and M. Reed, eds., *Oxford handbook of sociology, social theory and organization studies: Contemporary currents* (pp.510–533). Oxford University Press.

McGahan, A.M., 2019. My presidency of the academy of management: Moral responsibility, leadership, governance, organizational change, and strategy. *Journal of Management Inquiry*, *28*(3), pp.251–267.

McKinlay, A. and Starkey, K., eds., 1998. *Foucault, management and organization theory: From panopticon to technologies of self*. Sage.

McLeod, M.S., Payne, G.T. and Evert, R.E., 2016. Organizational ethics research: A systematic review of methods and analytical techniques. *Journal of Business Ethics*, *134*(3), pp.429–443.

McLynn, F., 2012. *The road not taken: How Britain narrowly missed a revolution*. Random House.

McNally, D., 2011. *Monsters of the market: Zombies, vampires and global capitalism*. Brill.

McSweeney, B., 2006. Are we living in a post-bureaucratic epoch? *Journal of Organizational Change Management*, *19*(1), pp.22–37.

Mehri, D., 2000. Death by overwork: Corporate pressure on employees takes a fatal toll in Japan. *Multinational Monitor*, *21*(6), p.26.

Metcalf, H.C. and Urwick, L., 2004. *Dynamic administration: The collected papers of Mary Parker Follett*. Routledge.

Milberg, W. and Amengual, M., 2008. *Economic development and working conditions in export processing zones: A survey of trends*. ILO.

Miller, P. and Rose, N., 2008. *Governing the present: Administering economic, social and personal life*. Polity.

Mills, C.W., 2001. *C. Wright Mills: Letters and autobiographical writings*. University of California Press.

Mills, J.H., Thurlow, A. and Mills, A.J., 2010. Making sense of sensemaking: The critical sensemaking approach. *Qualitative Research in Organizations and Management: An International Journal*, *5*(2), pp.182–195.

Mills, A.J. and Novicevic, M.M., 2019. *Management and organizational history: A research overview*. Taylor and Francis.

Milne, E., 1976. *No shining armour: The story of one man's fight against corruption*. John Calder, 1986.

Milne-Smith, A., 2011. Coffeehouses to clubhouses: Understanding the Gentlemen's Clubs of London. In *London Clubland* (pp.17–34). Palgrave Macmillan.

Morgan, G., 1986. *Images of organization*. Sage Publications.

Morgan, D.L., 2014. Pragmatism as a paradigm for social research. *Qualitative Inquiry*, *20*(8), pp.1045–1053.

Mouzelis, N.P., 2017. *Organization and bureaucracy: An analysis of modern theories*. Routledge.

Nandu-Templeton, J., Vanderklei, M., de Vries, H., Love, T. and Hamilton, R., 2017. Interpreting the narratives of Mäori entrepreneurs. *MAI Journal*, *6*(2), pp.164–179.

Nansubuga, F. and Munene, J.C., 2020. Awakening the Ubuntu episteme to embrace knowledge management in Africa. *Journal of Knowledge Management*, *24*(1), pp.105–119.

Nayak, A. and Chia, R., 2011. Thinking becoming and emergence: Process philosophy and organization studies. In H. Tsoukas and R. Chia, eds., *Philosophy and organization theory* (pp.281–309). Emerald Group Publishing Limited.

Negri, A., 2018. *From the factory to the metropolis: Essays volume 2*. John Wiley & Sons.

New Statesman, 1973. *The rule of omerta in Blyth constituency*. November 23, 1973.

Nicolini, D., 2013. *Practice theory, work, and organization: An introduction*. OUP

Nielsen, R.P., 2003. Corruption networks and implications for ethical corruption reform. *Journal of Business Ethics*, *42*(2), pp.125–149.

Nkomo, S.M., 2011. A postcolonial and anti-colonial reading of 'African' leadership and management in organization studies: Tensions, contradictions and possibilities. *Organization*, *18*(3), pp.365–386.

Norris, P., 2021. Cancel culture: Myth or reality? *Political Studies*, p.00323217211037023

Nove, A., 1977. Can Eastern Europe feed itself? *World Development*, *5*(5–7), pp.417–424.

Nybom, T., 2007. A rule-governed community of scholars: The Humboldt vision in the history of the European university. In Maassen, P. and Olsen, J.P. (eds.), *University dynamics and European integration* (pp.55–80). Springer.

Önnerfors, A., 2017. *Freemasonry: A very short introduction*. Oxford University Press.

Osland, A., 2020. *Gates/Buffet versus Bezos/Musk: Donate or invest?* Sage Publications: Sage Business Cases Originals.

Oswick, C., Fleming, P. and Hanlon, G., 2011. From borrowing to blending: Rethinking the processes of organizational theory building. *Academy of Management Review*, *36*(2), pp.318–337.

Oswick, C., Keenoy, T. and Grant, D., 2002. Note: Metaphor and analogical reasoning in organization theory: Beyond orthodoxy. *Academy of Management Review*, *27*(2), pp.294–303.

Ozanne, U.B. and Hunt, S.D., 1971. *The economic effects of franchising* (Vol. 1). US Government Printing Office.

Palmer, D., Biggart, N. and Dick, B., 2008. Is the new institutionalism a theory? In R. Greenwood, C. Oliver, T.B. Lawrence and R.E. Meyer, eds., *The Sage handbook of organizational institutionalism* (pp.739–768). Sage.

Parker, M., 2001. Fucking management: Queer, theory and reflexivity. *Ephemera*, *1*(1), pp.36–53.

Parker, M., 2008. Eating with the Mafia: Belonging and violence. *Human Relations*, *61*(7), pp.989–1006.

Parker, M., 2011. Organizing the circus: The engineering of miracles. *Organization Studies*, *32*(4), pp.555–569.

Parker, M., 2013. *Alternative business: Outlaws, crime and culture*. Routledge.

Parker, M., 2014. University, Ltd: Changing a business school. *Organization*, *21*(2), pp.281–292.

Parker, M., 2016. Secret societies: Intimations of organization. *Organization Studies*, *37*(1), pp.99–113.

Parker, M., 2018. *Shut down the business school*. University of Chicago Press Economics Books.

Parker, M., 2021. The critical business school and the university: A case study of resistance and co-optation. *Critical Sociology*, *47*(7–8), pp.1111–1124.

Parker, M., Fournier, V. and Reedy, P., 2008. *The dictionary of alternatives: Utopianism and organization*. Bloomsbury Publishing.

Parker, M., Cheney, G., Fournier, V. and Land, C., eds., 2014. *The Routledge companion to alternative organization*. Routledge.

Payan, T., 2016. *The three US-Mexico border wars: Drugs, immigration, and homeland security*. ABC-CLIO.

Peel, R., Patterson, A.H. and Gerlach, J.M., 2000. *Questions of English: Ethics, aesthetics, rhetoric, and the formation of the subject in England, Australia, and the United States*. Psychology Press.

Perry, P., Wood, S. and Fernie, J., 2015. Corporate social responsibility in garment sourcing networks: Factory management perspectives on ethical trade in Sri Lanka. *Journal of Business Ethics*, *130*(3), pp.737–752.

Peters, T. and Waterman, R.H., 1982. *In search of excellence*. Basic.

Pfeffer, J. and Salancik, G.R., 2003. *The external control of organizations: A resource dependence perspective*. Stanford University Press.

Powell, W.W. and DiMaggio, P.J., eds., 2012. *The new institutionalism in organizational analysis*. University of Chicago Press.

Pruijt, H., 1998. Multiple personalities: The case of business process reengineering. *Journal of Organizational Change Management*, *11*(3), pp.260–268.

Raffal, H., 2021. *Air power and the evacuation of dunkirk: The RAF and Luftwaffe during operation dynamo, 26 May–4 June 1940*. Bloomsbury Publishing.

Rawls, A.W., 2008. Harold Garfinkel, ethnomethodology and workplace studies. *Organization Studies*, *29*(5), pp.701–732.

Reed, M., 2010. Is communication constitutive of organization? *Management Communication Quarterly*, *24*(1), pp.151–157.

Reed, M., 2011. The post-bureaucratic organization and the control revolution. In S.R. Clegg, M. Harris and H. Höpfl (eds.), *Managing modernity: Beyond bureaucracy?* (pp.230–256). Oxford University Press.

Reed, M. and Burrell, G., 2019. Theory and organization studies: The need for contestation. *Organization Studies*, *40*(1), pp.39–54.

Reedy, P., 2002. Keeping the Black Flag flying: Anarchy, utopia and the politics of nostalgia. *The Sociological Review*, *50*(1), pp.169–188.

Ricoeur, P., 1979. The human experience of time and narrative. *Research in Phenomenology*, *9*, pp.17–34.

Robert, M., 2016. *Negotiating NAFTA*. University of Toronto Press.

Rometsch, M. and Sydow, J., 2006. On identities of networks and organizations-The case of franchising. *Advances in Organization Studies*, *20*, p.19.

Rose, N., O'Malley, P. and Valverde, M., 2006. Governmentality. *Annual Review of Law and Social Science*, *2*, pp.83–104.

Rowlinson, M., 1996. *Organisations and institutions: Perspectives in economics and sociology*. Macmillan International Higher Education.

Rowlinson, M., 1998. *Organizations and institutions*. Macmillan.

Rowlinson, M., 2004. Challenging the foundations of organization theory. *Work, Employment and Society*, *18*(3), pp.607–620.

Rowntree, 1940. Introduction to Metcalf, H.C. and Urwick, L., 2004. *Dynamic administration: The collected papers of Mary Parker Follett*. Routledge.

Sabuktay, A., 2009. Locating extra-legal activities of the modern state in legal-political theory: Weber, Habermas, Kelsen, Schmitt and Turk. *Crime, Law and Social Change*, *51*(5), pp.511–530.

Savickas, M.L., 2010. Career studies as self-making and life designing. *Career Research and Development*, *23*(23), pp.15–18.

Scheyvens, R., Banks, G., Meo-Sewabu, L. and Decena, T., 2017. Indigenous entrepreneurship on customary land in the Pacific: Measuring sustainability. *Journal of Management & Organization*, *23*(6), pp.774–785.

Schmidt, E., 1979. *The Sullivan principles: Decoding corporate camouflage*. Institute for Policy Studies.

Schofield, J., 2001. The old ways are the best? The durability and usefulness of bureaucracy in public sector management. *Organization*, *8*(1), pp.77–96.

Schumpeter, J., 1942. Creative destruction. *Capitalism, Socialism and Democracy*, *825*, pp.82–85.

Scott, R.W., Scott, W.R. and Meyer, J.W., 1994. *Institutional environments and organizations: Structural complexity and individualism*. Sage.

Scott, W.R., 1987. The adolescence of institutional theory. *Administrative Science Quarterly*, *32*(4), pp.493–511.

Scott, W.R., 2005. Institutional theory: Contributing to a theoretical research program. *Great Minds in Management: The Process of Theory Development, 37*(2), pp.460–484.

Scott, W.R., 2008. Approaching adulthood: The maturing of institutional theory. *Theory and Society, 37*(5), pp.427–442.

Scott-Cato, M. and Hillier, J., 2010. How could we study climate-related social innovation? Applying Deleuzean philosophy to transition towns. *Environmental Politics, 19*(6), pp.869–887.

Seabright, M.A. and Schminke, M., 2002. Immoral imagination and revenge in organizations. *Journal of Business Ethics, 38*(1), pp.19–31.

Selznick, P., 1948. Foundations of the theory of organization. *American Sociological Review, 13*(1), pp.25–35.

Selznick, P., 2011. *TVA and the grass roots: A study of politics and organization.* Quid Pro Books.

Shattock, M., 2000. *Managing modern universities.* Taylor & Francis.

Shenhav, Y., 1995. From chaos to systems: The engineering foundations of organization theory, 1879–1932. *Administrative Science Quarterly, 40*(4), pp.557–585.

Shenhav, Y.A., 2002. *Manufacturing rationality: The engineering foundations of the managerial revolution.* Oxford University Press.

Sikka, P., 2013. Why combatting tax avoidance means curbing corporate power: Prem Sikka shows how a tax avoidance industry has facilitated the corporate capture of UK policymaking. *Criminal Justice Matters, 94*(1), pp.16–17.

Sikka, P., 2015. No accounting for tax avoidance. *The Political Quarterly, 86*(3), pp.427–433.

Simpson, T.W., 2012. Evaluating google as an epistemic tool. *Metaphilosophy, 43*(4), pp.426–445.

Sims, R.R., 1991. The institutionalization of organizational ethics. *Journal of Business Ethics, 10*(7), pp.493–506.

Singh, J., 2017. *Unthinking mastery: Dehumanism and decolonial entanglements.* Duke University Press.

Smircich, L. and Calás, M.B., 1987. *Organizational culture: A critical assessment.*

Smith, J.S., 2006. *Building new deal liberalism: The political economy of public works, 1933–1956.* Cambridge University Press.

Smith, L.T., 2021. *Decolonizing methodologies: Research and indigenous peoples.* Bloomsbury Publishing.

Spender, J.C., 1996. Organizational knowledge, learning and memory: Three concepts in search of a theory. *Journal of Organizational Change Management, 9*(1), pp.63–78.

Spender, J.C. and Marr, B., 2005. A knowledge-based perspective. In B. Marr, ed., *Perspectives on intellectual capital* (pp. 183–195). Sage.

Spicer, A., 2017. *Business bullshit.* Routledge.

Spoelstra, S., 2005. Robert Cooper: Beyond organization. *The Sociological Review, 53*(1), pp.106–119.

Spratt, S., Simms, A., Neitzert, E. and Ryan-Collins, R., 2009. *The great transition.* New Economics Foundation.

Steffy, B.D. and Grimes, A.J., 1986. A critical theory of organization science. *Academy of Management Review, 11*(2), pp.322–336.

Strati, A., 1999. *Organization and aesthetics*. Sage.

Swedberg, R., 2003. Economic versus sociological approaches to organization theory. In H. Tsoukas and C. Knudsen, eds., *The Oxford handbook of organization theory* (pp.373–391). Oxford University Press.

Taylor, M.P., 2012. The entrepreneurial university in the twenty-first century. *London Review of Education, 10*(3), pp.289–305.

Taylor, J., 2021. *The Guardian*. October 5. www.theguardian.com/technology/2021/oct/05/facebook-outage-what-went-wrong-and-why-did-it-take-so-long-to-fix.

Tedeschi, J.T., ed., 2013. *Impression management theory and social psychological research*. Academic Press.

Thanem, T., 2001. Processing the body: A comment on Cooper. *Ephemera: Critical Dialogues on Organization, 1*(4), pp.348–366.

Thanem, T., 2004. The body without organs: Nonorganizational desire in organizational life. *Culture and Organization, 10*(3), pp.203–217.

Thanem, T., 2011. *The monstrous organization*. Edward Elgar Publishing.

Theilmann, J. and Cate, F., 2007. A plague of plagues: The problem of plague diagnosis in medieval England. *Journal of Interdisciplinary History, 37*(3), pp.371–393.

The new corporation: The unfortunately necessary sequel. Directors: Joel Bakan and Jennifer Abbott. Released 18 March 2021 (United Kingdom). Telefilm Canada.

Thomas, R. and Davies, A., 2005. What have the feminists done for us? Feminist theory and organizational resistance. *Organization, 12*(5), pp.711–740.

Thompson, J.D., 1956. On building an administrative science. *Administrative Science Quarterly, 1*, pp.102–111.

Thompson, P., 2013. Financialization and the workplace: Extending and applying the disconnected capitalism thesis. *Work, Employment and Society, 27*(3), pp.472–488.

Thompson, P. and Alvesson, M., 2005. Bureaucracy at work: Misunderstandings and mixed blessings. In P. Du Gay, ed., *The values of bureaucracy* (pp.121–140). Oxford University Press.

Todorov, T., 1984. *Mikhail Bakhtin: The dialogical principle*. Manchester University Press.

Torrez, F., 2011. La Via Campesina: Peasant-led agrarian reform and food sovereignty. *Development, 54*(1), pp.49–54.

Townley, B., 1997. The institutional logic of performance appraisal. *Organization Studies, 18*(2), pp.261–285.

Townley, B., 2002. The role of competing rationalities in institutional change. *Academy of Management Journal, 45*(1), pp.163–179.

Townley, B., 2008. *Reason's neglect: Rationality and organizing*. Oxford University Press.

Transparency International, 2021. *Corruption perceptions index*. www.transparency.org/en/cpi/2020/index/gbr.

Tseëlon, E., 1992. Is the presented self sincere? Goffman, impression management and the postmodern self. *Theory, Culture & Society, 9*(2), pp.115–128.

Tsing, A.L., 2011. *Friction: An ethnography of global connection*. Princeton University Press.

Tsing, A., 2012. Unruly edges: Mushrooms as companion species; for donna haraway. *Environmental Humanities*, *1*(1), pp.141–154.

Tsoukas, H. and Knudsen, C., eds., 2005. *The Oxford handbook of organization theory*. Oxford Handbooks.

Turner, B., 2004. Edward W. Said: Overcoming orientalism. *Theory, Culture & Society*, *21*(1), pp.173–177.

Turner, R.S., 2007. The 'rebirth of liberalism': The origins of neo-liberal ideology. *Journal of Political Ideologies*, *12*(1), pp.67–83.

Van der Ploeg, J.D., 2008. *The new peasantries: Struggles for autonomy and sustainability in an era of empire and globalization*. Earthscan.

Van der Ploeg, J., 2010. The peasantries of the twenty-first century: The commoditisation debate revisited. *The Journal of Peasant Studies*, *37*(1), pp.1–30.

Van de Ven, A.H. and Poole, M.S., 1995. Explaining development and change in organizations. *Academy of Management Review*, *20*(3), pp.510–540.

Van Maanen, J., Frost, P., Moore, P., Lundberg, C., Louis, M. and Martin, J., 1991. *The smile factory* (pp.58–76). Sage.

Van Meijl, T., 2000. Modern morals in postmodernity: A critical reflection on professional codes of ethics. *Cultural Dynamics*, *12*(1), pp.65–81.

Via Campesina, 2003. Food sovereignty. *Via Campesina*. January 2003

Vogel, R., 2012. The visible colleges of management and organization studies: A bibliometric analysis of academic journals. *Organization Studies*, *33*(8), pp.1015–1043.

Wedel, J.R., 1986. *The private Poland*. Facts on File Incorporated.

Weick, K.E., 1997. *Social psychology of organizing*. University of Chicago Press.

Weick, K.E., 2012. *Making sense of the organization, Volume 2: The impermanent organization* (Vol. 2). John Wiley & Sons.

Weick, K.E. and Roberts, K.H., 1993. Collective mind in organizations: Heedful interrelating on flight decks. *Administrative Science Quarterly*, *38*(3), pp.357–381.

Westwood, R. and Linstead, S., eds., 2001. *The language of organization*. Sage.

Whitley, R., 1987. Taking firms seriously as economic actors: Towards a sociology of firm behaviour. *Organization Studies*, *8*(2), pp.125–147.

Whitley, R., 1994. Dominant forms of economic organization in market economies. *Organization Studies*, *15*(2), pp.153–182.

Whitley, R., 1999. *Divergent capitalisms: The social structuring and change of business systems*. OUP.

Whyte, W.H., 2013. *The organization man*. University of Pennsylvania Press.

Williams, C.C., 2007. *Re-thinking the future of work: Directions and visions*. Macmillan International Higher Education.

Williams, K.S. and Mills, A.J., 2019. The problem with women: A feminist interrogation of management textbooks. *Management & Organizational History*, *14*(2), pp.148–166.

Williamson, O.E., 1993. Transaction cost economics and organization theory. *Industrial and Corporate Change*, *2*(2), pp.107–156.

Wilson, F.M., 2017. *Organizational behaviour and gender*. Routledge.

Wilson, J., 2013. "The devastating conquest of the lived by the conceived" the concept of abstract space in the work of Henri Lefebvre. *Space and Culture*, *16*(3), pp.364–380.

Windsor, D., 2016. BRIC multinational enterprises: The roles of corruption and nationalism. In R. van Tulder, A. Verbeke, J. Carneiro and M.A. Gonzalez-Perez, eds., *The challenge of Bric multinationals* (pp.145–160). Emerald Group Publishing Limited.

Wittfogel, K.S., 1957. *Oriental despotism: A comparative study of total power*. Yale University Press.

Wright, C., Nyberg, D., De Cock, C. and Whiteman, G., 2013. Future imaginings: Organizing in response to climate change. *Organization*, *20*(5), pp.647–658.

Yang, M. 1994. *Gifts, favours and banquets*. Cornell University Press.

Yunkaporta, T., 2019. *Sand talk: How Indigenous thinking can save the world*. Text Publishing.

Zuboff, S., 1988. *In the age of the smart machine*. Basic Books.

Zuboff, S., 2019. *The age of surveillance capitalism: The fight for a human future at the new frontier of power: Barack Obama's books of 2019*. Profile Books.

Zucker, L.G., 1987. Institutional theories of organization. *Annual Review of Sociology*, *13*(1), pp.443–464.

Index

and 73–74; power and 72–73;
process and 14–15; pyramidal
14, 33, 36; responsibility and 22;
structure and 14–15; time and
20–21; universities 67–69; *see also*
camouflage; entrepreneurialism;
large organizations
organizing 14–19, 21, 22, 23, 25, 69;
reflexive hermeneutics 63; *see also*
change
Organizing Outside Organizations
12–13
outsourcing 11, 33–34, 36

paraethics 39, 40
Parker, M. 4, 5
peasantry 55–60, 70–71; Organization
Theory's neglect of 61–62;
revolts 61
Peasant's Revolt of 1381 50
Philippines 46, 60
planning 21
platforms 13, 36
Pope, A. 14
Popper, K. 10
post-Fordism 45
Powell, W. W. 29
power 28, 35, 64, 67, 68, 72–73;
responsibility and 34
PPE (personal protective equipment) 9
practice 16, 23, 30
pragmatism 23, 27, 72
process 29; river metaphor 14, 19–20
Process Theory 15
proletariat 57, 60
pyramid structure 14, 33, 36

Rawls, A. 16
Reagan, R. 11
record keeping 55, 75
Reed, M. 66
Rees-Mogg, J. 15
reflexive hermeneutics 63
regimes of truth 25–26
regulation 45, 46, 74
resource and power dependency
theory 31
responsibility 22; franchises and 44;
large organizations and 33–34
Ricoeur, P., *Time and Narrative* 63

river metaphor 20
rule of law 54–55; *blat* and 55; corruption
and 48–49; World Justice Project
49–50; writing and 50–55
Russell Group 41
Russia 49; *blat* 51–53

Sartre, J.-P., *Being and Nothingness* 63
search engines 63
semiotics 17
senior management 14
serfdom 8; *see also* peasantry
Smircich, L. 17
social media 74; *see also* Facebook
social order 14, 15; *see also* order
social science 28, 34, 39
socialism 10–11
Soviet Union 10–11, 51–52
Spicer, A. 32
stasis 20
STEM 24, 28
structure 14–15, 29; pyramid 14, 33,
36; river metaphor 19
Sugar, A. 11
'surveillance capitalism' 39; *see also*
camouflage

Taylorism 60
text 17
Thailand 60
Thatcher, M. 11
time 20–21, 59; narrative temporality
(NT) 63
tolkach 52–53
Trump, D. 11, 27
truth 17; regimes of 25–26
Tsing, A. 21, 65–66
Tsoukas, H., *Organization Science* 15

Ubuntu 74
United Kingdom 11, 24, 28, 51, 73;
blat 54; Covid-19 9
United Nations 49
United States 10, 23, 28, 46, 54
universities 67–69, 73
University of Leicester 4
utterances 17

Van der Ploeg, J. D. 57, 59
Van Mannan, J. 40

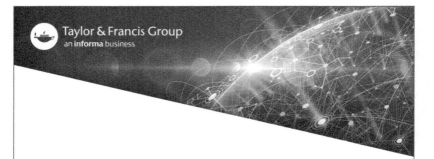